CRYPTOMANIA

KOBUS KLEYN CFP®

First published by Kobus Kleyn, April 2018

Copyright © 2018 by Kobus Kleyn

ISBN 978-1986689-40-3
Also available as an e-book

Cover design by Gregg Davies
www.greggdavies.com

Editor: Phillipa Mitchell

All rights reserved
The moral right of the author has been asserted

No part of this publication may be reproduced, distributed, or transmitted in any form or by any means, including photocopying, recording, or other electronic or mechanical methods, without the prior written permission of the author, except in the case of brief quotations embodied in critical reviews and certain other non-commercial uses permitted by copyright law.

Additional copies of this book can be purchased from all good bookstores worldwide.

Professional Waiver

This book was written with the intent to drive awareness and to educate the public and clients on cryptocurrencies and blockchain and should not be construed as advice of any nature or form. Neither should it be acted upon in any way without obtaining professional advice from reputable experts in the crypto industry, or financial professionals.

This publication has been written in my personal capacity and does not reflect the views of any company or entity that I may represent in any of my various capacities as a professional.

Kobus Kleyn CFP®

TABLE OF CONTENTS

	Introduction...	1
Chapter 1	Where did it all Begin?..	6
Chapter 2	Understanding the Difference between Fiat Currency and Bitcoin..	8
Chapter 3	Is Bitcoin a Bubble?..	13
Chapter 4	The Blockchain..	20
Chapter 5	Initial Coin Offerings (ICOs)................................	30
Chapter 6	A Case for Bitcoin?...	41
Chapter 7	Bitcoin: Strengths...	43
Chapter 8	Bitcoin: Weaknesses..	54
Chapter 9	Bitcoin: Opportunities...	76
Chapter 10	Bitcoin: Threats...	113
Chapter 11	Investing in Cryptocurrency: The SMART Analysis...	136
Chapter 12	Conclusion: A Summary of the SWOT and SMART Analysis..	144
Chapter 13	Are You Ready for Crypto-Conversations?	157
Chapter 14	Final Observations and Comments......................	168

INTRODUCTION

When Bitcoin started making headlines in South Africa in 2014, I had some concerns about this 'virtual digital currency', and I felt it only fair to begin driving awareness towards and education around the phenomenon.

My primary objective was to allow the public, my social media network, as well as my clients and fellow financial professionals in the financial planning profession to be able to make informed decisions before "biting into the coin". This then became the topic of my first major article on Bitcoin.

I wrote about Blockchain and Crypto Technology for the first time on the 19th of November 2014 under the heading, *Bitcoin: Bite the Coin or Not.*

My opinion on the subject has not changed since I wrote the article, and it will remain so until someone convinces me otherwise, regardless of the current volatility of Bitcoin and all various altcoins.

Some of the more serious questions that were asked in my 2014 article were:

- Could it be a speculative bubble?
- Could it be another Ponzi scheme?
- Could the future value of Bitcoin be valued or predicted?
- Could it become fatally flawed, with the designers not appreciating the integrated concept of money?
- Could Bitcoin maintain a sound financial establishment, or is it a threat to central banks, regulators and governments?
- Could Bitcoin become an investment risk for investors who might see other opportunities by speculating on the volatility of values, similar to buying long or short on the open stock markets? I do not even want to contemplate an EFT type fund and its associated risk.
- How would future government regulations across the world benefit or disadvantage the Bitcoin? Could it simply be banned or shut down?
- Could Bitcoin become a haven for criminal activities such as terrorism, cyber fraud with malware and the

loss of your "wallet" (even with cryptography technology), money laundering, and more?
- Could Bitcoin disadvantage economies by significantly driving "black market" activities?

In 2017, I decided to take my research over many years on cryptocurrency and turn it into a book. I have to admit that I did not anticipate the monster I had taken on when I embarked on gathering the material that I would use as the foundation for this book. It overburdened me tremendously, but I decided to tackle it head on and read and analyse as much as I could, over and above what I had done since.

This crypto monster from another dimension throws everything at a person. To select reputable articles out of the hundreds that are being generated on a daily basis from which to base my research is incredibly time-consuming. I stopped counting the articles after reaching the one-hundredth one.

Added to the mix is the most complex and challenging technology, terms and words, facts and fiction, hype and mania, sucker punches, believers and realists, and dreams and nightmares.

While writing this book, I decided to engage with other people on the subject matter as much as possible at conventions, seminars and the like.

I have endeavoured to keep this book as simple as possible for the man on the street. I would rather play devil's advocate at this stage of Bitcoin's ecosystem development, and crypto in general. This does not mean that I am not considering Bitcoin as a future "wonder of the world" which would significantly reduce consumer spending costs, giving billions of people who do not have access to modern banking facilities access to financial activities and transactions. I am also not excluding the possibility that Bitcoin could also become a future financial disaster.

I will not be a taking an official standpoint in this book in terms of purchasing cryptocurrency in its current form, although I will be testing and experiencing the different ecosystems for a short period by "investing in" Bitcoin so that I am able to write accurately on the subject matter.

I would only consider using and investing in cryptocurrency in the future if it becomes a regulated virtual currency or investment, and only if I had no other option to use it to purchase goods, or to trade.

My upfront tip to future Bitcoin users is as follows: *When you start using "virtual money" ask yourself whether you are willing to lose your "real" (fiat) money at any cost?*

Ultimately, it is up to the individual to decide whether they wish to partake in this new crypto ecosystem, and it is my hope that this book will allow for informed decisions to be made by the public and the consumer.

My hope is that the information I have recorded in this book will illustrate what I believe will one day become known as **Cryptomania**, the frontrunner to a new dimension of digital and virtual currencies in the world.

CHAPTER 1

WHERE DID IT ALL BEGIN?

As a Certified Financial Planner with fiduciary duties, I have been following the Bitcoin phenomenon since 2008 when a certain Satoshi Nakamoto (not a real person but rather a pseudonym) published a paper entitled "Bitcoin: a peer to peer electronic cash system" in which he referred to Bitcoin as a software-based online digital payment system. He was introduced to the public as a Japanese man born on 5 April 1975, credited with inventing and officially introducing Bitcoin and the blockchain to the world in January 2009.

It is understood that Satoshi Nakamoto was involved in the development of the source code until 2010 when it was handed over to Gavin Andersen. Nakamoto eventually pulled out of the Bitcoin project completely and disappeared.

At the time of writing and publishing this book, there is still no clarity on who the secret developers of Bitcoin and the blockchain are. In fact, it is probably the best-kept secret in the world when one considers the search prowess of the Internet, combined with the mass hysteria that surrounds Bitcoin.

We know that Sir Tim Berners-Lee, the creator of the World Wide Web, *at least* took credit for his part in its development over twenty years ago, but I find it interesting that "Satoshi Nakamoto" wishes to remain anonymous at a time when Bitcoin and the blockchain are thought to be one of the most significant events of the fourth Industrial Revolution. I have my own conspiracy theory around the 'secretive men in cloak' and the fact that the last finite Bitcoin will only be mined around 2140, but I will come back to this.

There is no doubt that whoever these "Satoshis" are that they must have some of the most incredible IQs in the world. To have come up with a blockchain design that prevents the double-spending of digital currencies (along with offering many more applications) required an astounding amount of combined brainpower.

There is a strong belief that these secret developers are actually cryptography and computer science experts mostly from the USA and Europe, and not of Japanese descent at all. This belief is realistic if we consider the strict financial regulatory controls in the USA and Europe.

CHAPTER 2

UNDERSTANDING THE DIFFERENCE BETWEEN FIAT CURRENCY AND BITCOIN

Fiat Currency

The term *"Fiat"* Currency originates from the Latin word meaning "It shall be" or "It will become". Fiat currency is a currency that holds no intrinsic value (for example, paper money) and is not backed by any commodity, such as gold or silver. The value of fiat money lies in the trust of those who hold it.

Fiat currency is not traded through an exchange of any kind. Instead, it is regulated by law or through government control.

Fiat money was used for the first time in China in 1000 AD. It is interesting to note that China has always had an impact on everything somewhere in the world. China, for instance, was the first country to officially ban ICOs (Initial Coin Offerings) and exchanges.

What is Bitcoin and how does it work?

Bitcoin was designed primarily as a Peer-to-Peer Electronic Cash System.

In the United States of America, Bitcoin is referred to by the US Treasury as a decentralised virtual currency, with certain media referring to it as "cryptocurrency" or digital currency.

In basic terms, Bitcoin payments are recorded in a public ledger that uses its own unit of account. These units are referred to as *Bitcoins*. The transfer of payments takes place without a central repository or administrator.

Being electronic in format, users have an "electronic wallet" to store their Bitcoins. This wallet is essentially a software wallet.

Bitcoin transactions work with a personal security key to prevent unauthorised transactions. If this complex key is lost, it is unrecoverable, meaning that you can kiss your Bitcoins goodbye forever. In the same 'token', it must be understood that Bitcoin currently lacks absolute consumer protection.

With the system being unregulated, Bitcoins can be stolen at any given time, and there is simply no refund system in place.

When a Bitcoin transaction is recorded, it is only linked to an electronic address. This may lead people to believe that payments made for goods and services using Bitcoin are anonymous. A merchant who accepts payment in the form of cryptocurrency will, in many cases, require the identity of the buyer in order to despatch an order, therefore invalidating this perceived anonymity. Over and above this, with Bitcoin being in the public domain, it is possible that despite the protection currently offered by the blockchain, future developments in technology and software could mean that identities are exposed.

The current debate over whether Bitcoin is a currency or simply a payment protocol will continue until clarification is obtained over how Bitcoin may or may not be able to meet the standard criteria in terms of what defines "money". Worldwide case law will define such criteria, along with determining a universally accepted term for this new form of "money". I suspect that the final outcome will be that Bitcoin - in its current form - will be classified as some type of commodity, but only time will tell. The bottom line is that it was always intended to be known as a currency, and if this does not happen, then it may simply fail in its objectives, and disappear.

Personally, I have no issues with virtual (digital) currencies in the long run, but only if they are regulated so as to ensure some sort of protection and as a means to hedge against fiat - or paper - currencies.

The question that comes to mind is whether, if crypto is neither a fiat currency nor is it based on something of tangible value such as gold, and even if it is only what people perceive it is worth, is it not simply 'monopoly money', at best?

There is a belief that fiat currency is no longer a legitimate store of value, and it is for this precise reason that the price of 'new generation' monies such as Bitcoin are achieving incredible values.

Prices may be increasing, but it does not mean that these cryptocurrencies are necessarily growing in value, as demonstrated by the experiences of people who purchased US real estate in 2007, or a Dutch tulip bulb between 1634 and 1637. The old saying of *what goes up must come down* should be kept in mind because nothing has historically ever followed a constant linear upward trend in growth. At the time of publishing this book, the value of Bitcoin is certainly on a downward trend.

With apologies to the younger generation who have no idea of what a telex machine is, but there was a time when the telex machine was overtaken by the fax machine. It was not all that long ago either that we were exposed to the idea of emails replacing fax machines.

How many of us still use faxes to communicate today? I am sure that in years to come, emails will be replaced by another means of direct electronic communications.

Similarly, could Bitcoin become the 'email' that replaces the hard (fiat) currency we have become so accustomed to? I hope that you will find the answer to this question while reading this book.

CHAPTER 3

IS BITCOIN A BUBBLE?

What do these events have in common?

- Tulip Mania (1634-1637)
- The South Sea Bubble (1716-1720)
- The Mississippi Bubble (1716-1720)
- The British Railway Mania bubble (the 1840s)
- The Florida Real Estate bubble (the 1920s)
- Kuwait's Souk al-Manakh stock bubble and crash (the 1980s)
- Japan's Bubble Economy (the 1980s)
- The Barings Bank collapse (1995)
- The Dot-com bubble (the 1990s)
- The Subprime Housing bubble (2008-2009)

All of these events were either hyped-up *get quick rich* schemes, or they were markets that were experiencing extraordinary escalations in *perceived* values.

The herd stampeded to join the party, but it did not end well. The bubble, scheme or market eventually imploded - catastrophically - and millions of people lost their fortunes.

George Bernard Shaw once said, *"We learn from history that we learn nothing from history."*

When will we learn that the impossible does not happen, and that when it sounds too good to be true, why should we expect it to be true?

Economic Bubbles

A soap bubble has no innate substance, yet it has the ability to rise in thin air. It rises and falls with each gentle breeze, but with nothing of substance to keep it intact it will eventually pop under atmospheric pressure and dissipate into the breeze.

Economic bubbles, similarly, are phenomena that are directly linked to people's emotional behaviour. They occur when 'investors' beliefs and demands push asset pricing beyond any rational reflection of what such asset is worth in real terms, with no or very little intrinsic value. When valuations cannot be performed (or even calculated in any format that makes viable sense), the bubble grows in size until it can no longer sustain itself, and eventually bursts.

Crypto may be following the classic bubble stages, and, if Bitcoin does in fact crash, it could be the 'mother' of all crashes, together with that of her altcoin offspring. Word of a possible crash has been on many people's lips in 2017 and 2018, with the spike in the crypto bubble chart appearing to be a classic example of the hype before the flatline. The question remains whether crypto is a bubble building and waiting to pop, or not.

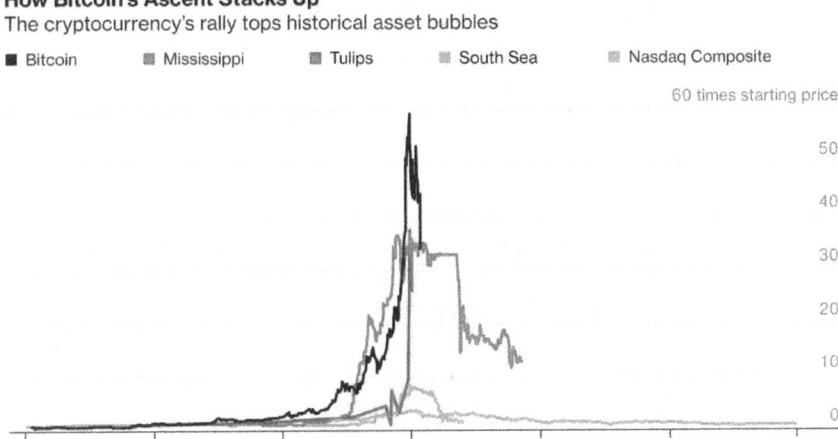

The graph above demonstrates the classic trends of some of the major bubbles (such as the Dutch tulip bulb market bubble) and compares them to the current stage of Bitcoin. As you will see, it does reflect a concerning historical trend. If Bitcoin is indeed a bubble, it will most certainly dwarf the original tulip bulb mania of four hundred years ago, becoming by far the largest bubble ever to pop, forever recorded in our history books as *The Mother of all Bubbles*.

The interesting thing about bubbles is what you get from them. In the case of the tulip bulb bubble, at least you got a tulip, but with the Bitcoin bubble, you have nothing to show, other than, perhaps, a number to your Bitcoin.

There is only one guaranteed outcome for greed-driven manias, and that is an implosion in price, leading to major losses that ultimately disappear into a dark hole.

Regulation should help control some of the obvious greed drivers when speculators, amateur economists and investors caught in a herd mentality begin to stampede.

Crypto may or may not be following the same pattern, but it could implode as soon as the perfect storm hits. Two factors which may contribute towards this implosion are:

- The formation of blockchain bottlenecks
- Too many coins (altcoins) in the open market

Other factors will be discussed later in this book.

The altcoins to Bitcoin (of which there are currently 1500+) would be the immediate casualties. One of the main reasons why I feel that cryptocurrencies - in their current form and use - could indeed be the mother of all bubbles in the making, is because as long as four hundred years ago and as recent as twenty years ago, communication, as we know it today, did not exist.

Today we have the Internet, social media and various other electronic communication platforms that have been adopted on a massive scale by people all over the world. As such, communication takes place in *real time* – often instantly and en masse – and therefore, if this is indeed a 'bubble', and with the heated undercurrent of social media driving hype and the herd effect, then we could be in for the mother of all bubbles.

I would like to refer to the social media impact phenomenon as FLIGHT. This acronym is made up of:

- **F**acebook
- **L**inkedIn
- **I**nstagram
- **G**oogle
- **H**ootSuite, and
- **T**witter

When people talk about a phenomenon *en masse*, perceptions and perceived value can become massively powerful, even if it is all in the mind and underpinned by emotions. The FOMO (Fear Of Missing Out) impact can never be underestimated.

Current day active and virtual communication tools and technology will be driving this 'bubble' with a great deal of heated undercurrent, taking the coin to levels never seen before. Altitude will eventually pop the bubble, and social media will most certainly aid in ensuring that the bubble crashes back to Earth a great deal faster than it drifted upwards, should it indeed be a bubble.

This concern was clearly picked up by Facebook when they banned all marketing and adverts for cryptocurrencies (including Bitcoin) and ICOs. With Google following suit - and possibly even Twitter - many of the core ingredients of the 'Flight' acronym are falling away, with it becoming more and more difficult to maintain altitude.

It is interesting to note that the majority of subscribers to crypto's official news site, CoinDesk, are of the view that there may be a bubble in cryptocurrencies. A recent survey conducted by CoinDesk found that close to 60% of its readers believe that digital assets are in a bubble. Close to

70% of the readers surveyed are investors themselves, which could be dangerous if they lost confidence and all sold out at once. You can find more information in the CoinDesk Q2 *State of the Blockchain Report* on their website at coindesk.com

Cryptomania vs Kleptomania

When I stumbled across the word Kleptomania (*klep-toe-MAY-nee-uh*) while researching the title of this book, I wondered if cryptomania was not possibly an offshoot of this impulsive mental health disorder that overwhelms the sufferer with an irresistible urge to steal. When one considers how the crypto professionals (who know mostly when to take their profits) are promoting Bitcoin knowing full well that it is extremely volatile in nature and that newcomers to the market could lose their fortunes if they blindly enter the market without any prior knowledge of its workings, cryptomania is, in some way, a form of theft; and certainly a theft of common sense, built on a solid foundation of hype.

Whether there is any correlation between cryptomania and kleptomania remains, of course, to be seen, but the current mania surrounding crypto certainly seems to be driving the most logical of human beings to risk everything in the hope of amassing great fortunes, with little consideration to the possible downsides.

CHAPTER 4

THE BLOCKCHAIN

The blockchain is a decentralised, publicly distributed digital ledger for financial transactions. The blockchain serves as a public ledger for all coin transactions that have ever been made.

Crypto is built on the foundation of the blockchain and is probably just Phase 1 (or Blockchain 1.0) of what is possible with the blockchain in general.

Although the blockchain was designed to operate Bitcoin, the blockchain does not need Bitcoin to justify itself as a technology. Bitcoin, however, cannot function without the blockchain, but it appears that Bitcoin evangelists certainly abuse the credentials of blockchain technology to boost the 'trust' levels of Bitcoin. It is a bit of a chicken-and-egg situation.

The blockchain does not store personal information, but it does store each transaction complete with its date, the time of the transaction, and its value. It is completely transparent, secure and streamlined with little involvement from third parties.

Transactions are captured in limited data blocks, and, once a block is filled to maximum capacity with transactions, it is added to the end of the 'chain' in sequential order, upon which a new block comes into play.

Although the blockchain is currently used to chronologically record (mainly) Bitcoin and altcoin transactions, there is no doubt that it could be - and will be - used for many other financial applications in the near future. Blockchain technology is transforming and evolving even as you read this book.

Besides being used as both an instrument of finance, and as a means of facilitating smart contracts (discussed later in this book), blockchain technology has many other practical uses. The blockchain can play a major role in legitimising voting systems, ensuring that voting records are accurate and that the results are not manipulated. With the Trump voting saga in the USA, and other voting irregularities across the globe, the blockchain could be used as a sound and secure vote-counting system that secures every vote into a ledger that, once counted, cannot be tampered with. *Follow My Vote* (followmyvote.com) is one such startup company that is pioneering the idea.

Humanitarian work with refugees can be supported through blockchain technology, with cryptocurrency vouchers being used to buy food. Ethereum technology, for example, can minimise bureaucracy delays by facilitating direct donations to organisations supporting the welfare of international refugees.

The poorest of the poor can benefit tremendously from blockchain technology through financial vouchers for people who do not have formal bank accounts; they would simply need access to a smartphone. A great example of such a platform is BitPesa, a company that is creating economic freedom for the impoverished in Africa with cheaper money transfer options. They are also helping people to find business value in faraway countries.

Blockchain has huge efficiency opportunities, especially in countries with *inefficient* governments, especially when it comes to enhancing efficiencies in healthcare, education and other public utilities.

Other blockchain uses currently under development include blockchain financial services, cyber security, car leasing and vehicle sales, insurance claim processing, smart appliances, and passport and birth certificate controls, to name but a few.

The Blockchain Process

The blockchain process is made up of the following elements:

- A **Transaction** - This is technical and complex in nature, and signals the blockchain;

- A **Block** – This is simply a list of transactions that also functions to prevent double payments;

- **Miners** – Miners mine the algorithms and confirm legitimate transactions. They receive both newly-mined Bitcoins (and, in some cases, fees) for their efforts;

- **Merchants** – Merchants accept the validations from the miners;

- **Coin transfers** – These occur either as full coins or in bits of coins known as *Satoshis*. A Satoshi, the smallest unit of a Bitcoin, represents a hundred millionth of a Bitcoin.

With Satoshis, anyone can afford to buy into Bitcoin (the proposed people's currency) at a fraction of the value of a full coin. If you happened to have purchased some

Satoshi- even the smallest fraction - in 2009 when it had no significant price level, and you held onto it (instead of using it for its intended purpose of making payment for goods), you would have been very wealthy today.

Every step of the blockchain process has huge technical challenges with an inherent complexity, not only for the man on the street but also for the designers, the miners and the believers.

What is mining?

Cryptocurrency mining delivers two primary functions:

- Adding transactions to the blockchain by securing and verifying transactions

- Releasing new currency into the ecosystem through bitcoin blocks

The mining itself takes place using special software programs on powerful computers. This software performs extensive and expensive calculations (the mining process) to create a block on the blockchain. The blocks that are mined must contain proof-of-work. Proof-of-work is a way of identifying and verifying a miner by requiring the miner to satisfy certain requirements, for example by solving a puzzle that requires a serious amount of computational effort before they can actually begin mining.

During the mining process, the miners go up against each other to solve complex mathematical algorithms in an effort to verify transactions as quickly as possible. In order to solve these algorithms, miners use cryptographic hash functions to hunt for a hash value. The first miner to crack the algorithm and verify the transaction claims the block and receives the (current) reward of 12.5 bitcoins.

In earlier years you would only find cryptography experts and enthusiasts operating as miners due to Bitcoin's low value, but as Bitcoin's value increased, mining became a lucrative business, with many new miners joining the mining clubs by purchasing their own hardware.

The computing resources associated with mining are huge. Many computers are stacked on top of each other and require efficient cooling systems to prevent them from overheating, unless you are mining in Iceland - or any other country with a cold climate - where the ambient temperature does the job effectively without the need for additional cooling systems.

The Blockchain and its potential

Blockchain 2.0 will run contract applications and Blockchain 3.0 could run distribution application models and so Blockchain 4.0 etc. will follow and transform into a completely new technological ecosystem.

It appears that there are simply no limitations to the blockchain. It certainly does not require much effort on my part (or that of anyone else) to make a case for it, especially when one considers that it occupies a long-term, viable place in the fourth industrial revolution, if it does not become a revolution *on its own*. I have been unable to find even one negative concern to contradict its existence. In fact, the blockchain seems to have the potential of the 'Internet-of-Things' (IoT) that began over twenty years ago[1]. Back then, despite the fact that it was the most profound technological invention, most people thought that it was simply another craze or mania. Today, the number of devices with an on/off switch that can be connected to the Internet (and/or to each other), is steadily growing. *The Internet of things*[2], in hindsight, was most certainly not a fad.

---

[1] *I am not trying to compare the blockchain to the Internet; I am using it purely as an example on what is possible.*

[2] *Also known as IoT, it is the interconnection of computing devices, via the Internet, enabling them to send and receive data.*

My belief is that the average man on the street does not know the difference between blockchain and bitcoin (and other crypto coins) and where the dependency lies. This lack of knowledge is well-utilised by the believers as a means of giving Bitcoin and crypto a strong and immediate element of integrity and trustworthiness.

Similarly, even so-called experts who do not believe in the sustainability of current cryptocurrencies do believe that the blockchain is here to stay, and that it will disrupt current financial transactions and financial institutions and its related entities. As I have stated before, crypto needs the blockchain in order to operate successfully, but the blockchain does not need crypto per se.

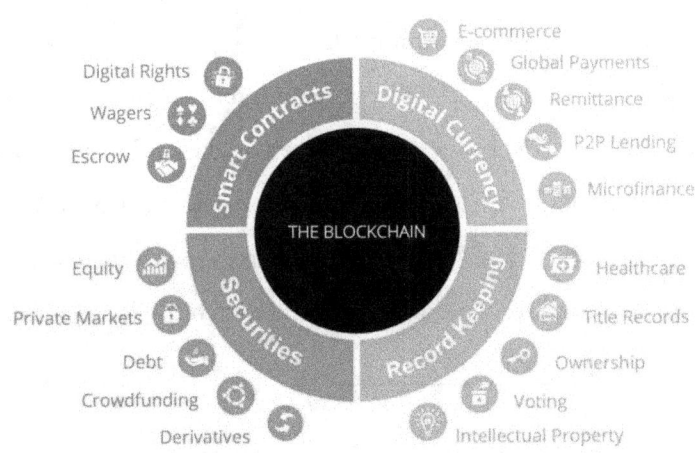

The infographic[3] above depicts the blockchain's potential perfectly:

The blockchain - and its underlying technology - has huge potential to disrupt many industries that contain an economic surplus. With the open source nature of the public blockchain protocols, this economic surplus can be transferred to the people and aid in breaking down monopolies that are controlled by intermediaries and middlemen.

I believe that blockchain technology will become a major disruptor during the fourth Industrial Revolution. Because of its high level of encryption integrity, the blockchain is driving the use of (and belief in) Bitcoin (and other cryptocurrencies) more than anything else. There is no doubt that it could be (and will be) used for many other financial applications in the near future, as mentioned previously.

For the time being, the blockchain serves the main purpose of a public ledger for all coin transactions that have ever been made. The transactions are captured in limited data blocks, and as the block fills up to maximum capacity, it is added to the end of the 'chain' in sequential order, with a new block coming into play. The blockchain does not store personal

---

[3] *Source: Adrenaline Agency*

information, but it does store every single transaction with a date, a time and the transaction amount. It is transparent, secure and streamlined, and involves very few third parties.

As the blockchain evolves within its own ecosystem (beyond cryptocurrency use), it will be seen as an incorruptible, transparent recordkeeping platform which bypasses regulatory censorship. The blockchain has the ability to eradicate institutional, government and financial corruption, and could, therefore, protect the human rights of individuals in a global society, as well as ensure that taxpayer's money is used effectively.

The greatest threat to blockchain technology could be the potentially bad reputation it could attract due to its direct link to Bitcoin and other cryptocurrencies, and especially if any of them fail.

CHAPTER 5

INITIAL COIN OFFERINGS (ICOs)

Anybody can create a new cryptocurrency, but funds are required in order to make it. A venture capitalist investor would expect some form of ownership in a company in return for their investment, but ICOs are a way around this. ICOs are, in essence, the virtual alternative to the venture capital (VC) methods of investment that many of us are familiar with.

ICOs are a popular crowdfunding method of raising capital for new blockchain-based assets. Individuals would send the new cryptocurrency creator 'money' in the form of well-established cryptocurrencies like Bitcoin or Ethereum, or even fiat currencies like the US Dollar, in exchange for these new tokens. The transaction is a gamble for the crowd funder because the value of the new token could go either way.

In 2017, crypto ICO listings generated more than three times the value of combined – traditional - Venture Capital transactions, and in many cases more than a single VC transaction.

It is possible that ICOs could replace VCs (in part) in the future because the mechanism opens the early finance stages of a project to the wider investment market with access to a larger volume of people who would not have access to such facilities under normal circumstances.

In 2017, China and its seven financial regulators took a draconian view and banned ICOs in the country, declaring them illegal. The regulators stated that they believed crypto token sales to be unauthorised, with concerns that they would lead to illegal public funding and financing. They were of the belief that ICOs could drive financial crimes in different forms, including fraud, pyramid and Ponzi schemes, resulting in innocent people throwing money into quick money making schemes.

With many celebrities becoming ambassadors for cryptocurrencies, the government could see cryptomania spinning out of control and hence the larger problem of ICOs. This problem is not unique to China, with many other countries following suit in terms of their regulations surrounding ICOs.

China has gone as far as insisting that ICO funding will have to be repaid to the original funders.

China and its many financial regulators believe that the country is being abused by the miners, who use the cheap hydroelectricity systems available to them to drive the price of crypto coins upwards.

China's intentions are clear, and it comes as no surprise for a country that enjoys full state control over its people, with a president who now can serve for an unlimited period. With crypto being an international 'currency', it is certain that China would lose a significant amount of their state control. Declaring all ICOs illegal, regardless of their standing in the financial securities arenas, would give the government time to rectify matters in the best interests of the country, protect its citizens, and possibly even issue their own cryptocurrency.

Other countries are following suit. In the USA, the U.S. Securities and Exchange Commission (SEC) is considering banning cryptocurrencies after differentiating between coins that trade in unregistered securities from other coins that trade more like tokens. They are also informing so-called 'exchanges' to register as official exchanges under the SEC, so as to prevent misrepresentation as a formal exchange.

In September 2017 the US regulator declared that ICOs, token sales and crowd sales will be subject to the requirements of federal securities laws, further stating that they believed ICO's to be disrupting the financial order and economies of countries. This is certain to pull back the horse bolting on ICOs and, with China, India and USA having always been targeted as huge players in the crypto market due to the sheer size of their consumer market, it is, therefore, possible that ICOs could reach extinction before VCs do.

Both major economies (China and the USA) have stated clearly that they are not against *blockchain technologies* per se, and that they will encourage the adoption of such technology on its merits as a future game changer in financial services. The blockchain could disrupt the formal, regulated, financial industry as a whole. After ICOs were banned in China, the value of cryptocurrencies took a severe tumble. It is however not unusual for coins to take a knock in general – as had been demonstrated in recent years – and it should be noted that many cryptocurrencies have proved to Be resilient and have come back every time thus far.

Cybercrime

The growth in the number of cyber criminals who were reported to have scammed at least 10% of all capital from

ICOs through phishing schemes in 2017 alone does not bode well for ICOs if they are to be deemed trustworthy.

As a financial planner, I can only warn the public against these phishing scams. Phishers have found a new feeding ground and will come at you in full force. The same goes for criminal opportunists who will use the crypto hype to design pyramid and Ponzi schemes under the Bitcoin and other crypto banners, catching many in the early FOMO stages.

As recently as March 2018, one such Ponzi scheme (currently under investigation by the South African Hawks) was unearthed with more than 27 500 'investors' involved, including South Africans, Americans and Australians. The company in question is BTC global. Bitcoins to the value of over $50 million was transferred into an online wallet address for the Ponzi scheme.

Celebrities like Floyd Mayweather, who, in my opinion, has had a knock or two too many to the head, and Paris Hilton (for those who can remember her) are putting millions into *hot cryptos*. This is no doubt good news for the miners, together with a signal to build new and ongoing integrity and awareness around coin sales.

With all the bad news driving cryptocurrency price volatility, a good news story is always a breath of fresh air to aid in the recovery process. One such good news story is that Britain's 'Bra Baroness' and founder of the lingerie company Ultimo, Michelle Mone (in partnership with her boyfriend, Douglas Barrowman), is offering apartments in their new $326 million Dubai Tower for sale to the Bitcoin community.

This was a first in the world for residential property. The forty-storey apartment building should sell out quickly considering the thousands of crypto-millionaires out there wondering how to lighten their e-wallets and turn some of their millions into physical assets. Of course, this is until the bubble becomes too heavy to be sustained and the 'Bra Baroness' may find herself requiring a Wonderbra to keep things up.

The question remains in terms of where cryptocurrencies are really going, especially when one considers how much effort many governments are making at finding ways to regulate it, or banning them completely if they cannot be regulated.

The coin believers – also known as crypto evangelists, or crypto revolutionaries - and especially the original Bitcoin believers, have no doubt (and cannot be convinced otherwise) that Bitcoin will ultimately overthrow the regulated financial systems in most countries and replace fiat currencies. They want central banks to be destroyed and fiat currencies to go for a drive off a cliff. Bitcoin and Ethereum want to do away with banks, lawyers and anyone who might be 'stealing' the believer's money in order to line their own pockets. The believers predict a new world order in which blockchain technology will be the primary method of transacting, and Bitcoin the primary currency used.

Crypto and blockchain survey

Before we move onto the next chapter, let us analyse the results of a survey that I conducted in 2017.

The following ten questions were posed to the open public on LinkedIn (including my following of over 20 000 connections), and they were answered as follows:

Do you know about the blockchain?

- 86% Yes
- 14% No

This was a positive response, hopefully indicative of an awareness of both the blockchain and Bitcoin as separate entities.

Do you understand blockchain technology?

- 54% Yes
- 46% No

The "yes" results were higher than anticipated, considering the fact that I spent many months studying it in considerably more detail than the average man on the street.

Do you know about Bitcoin?

- 98% Yes
- 2% No

This is a clear indication that Bitcoin is indeed a household name after stealing the limelight in 2017.

Do you understand Bitcoin?

- 70% Yes
- 30% No

This result was higher than expected, but perhaps the question could have been phrased more technically.

Do you know about altcoins (cryptocurrencies)?

- 67% Yes
- 33% No

This was a surprising outcome as I certainly did not expect such a high percentage of "yes" responses.

Do you own any altcoins?

- 18% Yes
- 82% No

This outcome was expected, especially when one considers that there are over 1500 altcoins currently on the market.

If you own altcoins, which do you own?

- Bitcoin
- Ethereum
- Bitcoin Cash
- Ripple
- Litecoin
- NEO
- GRS
- XTH
- XEM
- LOTA
- IOTA
- GOLEM
- MONERO
- DASH
- Expanse
- LSK
- ICash

Most of the respondents indicated that they held Bitcoin, Ethereum and Bitcoin Cash. Bitcoin was ticked every time, with only a small percentage of respondents holding more than one type of coin.

What do you believe Bitcoin (crypto) to be?

- A currency?
  44.4%

- An asset class?
  9.09%

- An investment?
  6.06%

- A Ponzi scheme?
  5.05%

- A pyramid scheme?
  4.04%

- A phenomenon?
  5.05%

- A purchasing tool?
  14.14%

- A bit of a 'con'?
  3.03%

- The *Internet of things* of twenty years ago?
  0%

- A bubble?
  9.09%

It is clear that the majority of respondents see Bitcoin as a currency and not as an asset, even though they are using it as an asset and not a currency; a major breach of the Bitcoin

White Paper. Only 9% of respondents believe – or want to believe – that Bitcoin is not a bubble.

Do you believe the blockchain is -

- The *Internet of things* of twenty years ago? 7.07%
- A future technology? 25.25%
- A disruptor to financial services? 43.43%
- Here to stay? 22.22%
- The best thing ever? 2.02%

The majority of respondents see the blockchain as a disruptor to the financial and banking industry, with many hoping that it is here to stay.

CHAPTER 6

A CASE FOR BITCOIN?

Now that I have covered one side of the coin, I will focus on a possible case *for* cryptocurrencies.

Since the beginning of 2017, there has been a significant increase in hype on all media platforms on the most topical subject matter we have seen in decades and across all borders of the world where internet is prevalent and even if not.

I decided to put to work years of high level corporate, business and entrepreneurial skills and expertise, combined with logic, economics, markets, currency and financial experience and inclusive of my CFP®, TEP™ and TP™ designations, as well as my membership to nine affiliations and professional bodies - SAIT, FPI, FIA, FISA, STEP, MDRT, ISSA, The Institute of Ethics, and Unashamedly

Ethical - and create a framework to evaluate the Bitcoin using the basis of an SWOT analysis.

I will go into detail on each aspect of this SWOT analysis in the following chapters (with some in more detail than others) and conclude my analysis with some SMART outcomes and a final executive conclusion.

CHAPTER 7

BITCOIN: STRENGTHS

Before the SWOT purists have a go at me, allow me to state that I am well aware that strengths and weaknesses come from within, and opportunities and threats from without. I have not focussed on this, but rather the content and the message.

You will notice that I have had a little fun with this SWOT analysis by using the letters that make up each aspect of the analysis (namely, *Strengths*, *Weaknesses*, *Opportunities*, and *Threats*) and using them as acronyms. Each letter that makes up a word will have a detailed explanation alongside it.

Let us begin with the strengths associated with the blockchain, starting with the letter 'S'.

Software

The blockchain software has been designed with the objective of no human touch (in theory) to ensure trustworthiness and integrity. It is, however, software that must be written *by* a human being with the help of a computer program that is designed to automatically verify and transfer value globally, and, as such, it is therefore still open to abuse.

Blockchain software has strong integrity and appears to be highly trusted because of its technology backbone. The software has not been stress-tested yet, but this will most certainly happen in the future as the value of Bitcoin escalates, as competitors and alternative cryptocurrencies enter the market, and as enhanced technologies that use alternative mining software to validate transactions come into play.

Transportable

Bitcoin is highly transportable and operates without borders, supporting Bitcoin's transnationality. With an arm's length approach between parties, Bitcoin transactions allow for privacy and anonymity, supported by excellent system functionality.

Regulations

Bitcoin's decentralisation strategy should, and could be, one of Bitcoin's most effective strengths due to its efforts to restrict governmental and institutional interference.

This could, however, also be a threat – discussed later in Chapter 10 (*Bitcoin: Threats*) – in that what might be its alliance for long-term sustainability could also be its Achilles heel, as governments decide to regulate it.

Clarity around its regulation is essential in order to lift the regulatory fog that is building up amongst many countries globally.

Enigma

When something is mysterious or difficult to understand, and it is surrounded by a cloak of secrecy, it becomes an enigma. When it all starts with a creator or a developer with a pseudonym like Satoshi Nakamoto, the individual genius or group of geniuses who came up with the blockchain and Bitcoin technology, it is easy to pique people's interest.

The Bitcoin enigma is really a case of a solution requiring a problem. The problem presented itself conveniently in 2008 with the subprime crisis, starting in the USA and then spreading globally like a virus.

Bitcoin's enigmatic character drives awareness towards it through hype, while simultaneously protecting it through resilience and momentum.

Neutral

The Bitcoin system has a great deal of neutrality at its disposal: It supposedly requires no middlemen or intermediaries; (theoretically) has low costs and good security; it operates outside of geographic borders; and it reduces government and institutional intervention while allowing for complex, decentralised transactions. These concepts will, however, be stress-tested as the ecosystem evolves, with the jury still being out on the effectiveness of some of the key drivers mentioned.

One of Bitcoin's key (original) principles was that there would be no middlemen involved, and the primary reason for this would be to keep transaction costs and fees to a minimum. The opposite is proving to be true in reality, however. I am of the opinion that middlemen do in fact exist – in the form of miners.

Without the miners, it would not be possible to validate transactions. When Bitcoin mining first began, the successful miner would receive a reward of 50 Bitcoins per block. With its first halving, this commission dropped down to 25 Bitcoins per block, and then down to 12.5 Bitcoins per block, as it currently stands.

The rewards will continue to reduce until it eventually hits zero when the last Bitcoin is mined around 2140. The fees, however, will continue to escalate over time as the miner's rewards reduce in size and, in my opinion, will become unaffordable once there are only fee rewards for the miners, and no Bitcoins. There will be some serious stress-testing at this point, but bear in mind that this will only take place 122 years in the future.

Gold

Many refer to Bitcoin as 'Virtual Gold' because of its limited quantity, and some would like it to be a commodity. There is even a coin that goes by the name Bitcoin Gold.

There are only twenty-one million Bitcoins that can be mined in total. This 'finite' quality will lead to a perceived scarcity of the coin, similar to gold where there are only a certain quantity of deposits in the world. The Bitcoin rush might even be comparable to the 1855 Gold Rush in South Africa.

With the value of Bitcoin having increased exponentially, every effort has been made to build integrity by having Bitcoin placed in the same league as gold by the miners and the believers who make up a critical part of the Bitcoin ecosystem. Bitcoin, however, has seven times the *volatility* of gold. Because of its simplicity, gold is seen as a store of value, while Bitcoin, with all its complexity, would struggle to justify itself as a 'store of value'.

One of the most important reasons why Bitcoin is not comparable to gold is because gold is a commodity with an actual use. Sixty percent of all gold is used in the manufacturing of jewellery. Although Bitcoin is used as a unit of exchange, seven percent of its owners - at best - are using it for transactional purposes; certainly no mass usage at all.

On 3 March 2017 (at then-current price levels) Bitcoin, for the first time in history, became more expensive than an ounce of gold. Perhaps the believers are indeed onto something. But, as a gold investor, would you take slivers from your gold bar to exchange it for a cup of coffee at Starbucks? Similarly, would you use a Satoshi of your Bitcoin to do the same?

Bitcoin has become somewhat of a crypto monster to categorise. It cannot be compared to gold, but it could resemble a currency in some form especially when it is used to make payments rather than being a store of value. Either way, Satoshi Nakamoto referred to Bitcoin as 'electronic cash', with cash being intrinsically liquid. It cannot be classified as a share or a stock, unless we take ICOs into consideration. At best it resembles an unintended asset class in some form. Bitcoin, in fact, exhibits similar behaviours to all three of these categories at different times, which creates a great deal of confusion in terms of categorisation.

Harvard and Yale students have been unable to define Bitcoin under any economic theory or principle, and are still scratching their heads over it. In theory, monetary transactions operate on the basis of an exchange of a commodity for credit. When a bank creates money, it is inherently creating debt. Because no regulator, government or institution is backing the Bitcoin or its technology as yet, mined Bitcoins are technically free of debt. If debtors are not backing this so-called 'currency', then how is its value determined?

Attempting to categorise Bitcoin within any of these principles would mean that Bitcoin would be classified as worthless because it is created out of thin air, from nothing.

Is the value coming from the fact that believers are not using Bitcoins as a payment vehicle, but holding (or *holdling*) on to them? *Hodl* is a slang term used by the Bitcoin community and was 'coined' in 2013 by an inebriated Bitcoin guru participant in an online forum who posted, "I am hodling". People reading the post thought he was using the acronym

Hold on for Dear Life, but it was a drunken typo, and the word stuck.

JPMorgan Chase CEO, Jamie Dimon, took a shot at Bitcoin on CNBC in 2017, stating that the cryptocurrency "…is a fraud…", that "…It's just not a real thing; eventually, it will be closed", and that, "It's worse than tulip bulbs. It won't end well. Someone is going to get killed."

At a banking industry conference organised by Barclays in the same year, he stated, "Currencies have legal support. It (Bitcoin) will blow up…"

It will still be some time before we know who is right and who is wrong, but there *will* be a final outcome, even if it is close to 2140 when the last coin is mined and issued. I am of the opinion that the answers will be revealed long before that, and certainly in my lifetime.

Timely

The timing of the Fourth Industrial Revolution (also known as the digital revolution), combined with a search for an alternative to centralised control after the 2008/2009 economic meltdown of markets (due to the banking industry's abuse of subprime) brought about a perfectly timed storm to announce Bitcoin's arrival. Little can stop an idea if its time has arrived, and this is unquestionably relevant when we consider the blockchain, Bitcoin, and future cryptocurrencies with their intended objectives; the primary one being the use of Bitcoin as a transaction tool.

Hype

Generating hype (awareness) from nothing within a global environment was a complex matter two decades ago, before the *Internet of things*. Social media has placed 'hype' at our fingertips, and this same hype has frequently been compounded by fake news.

The herd factor requires hype to drive its momentum. Volume and value (quantity and price) can be driven by emotional hype (FOMO) and the perception of great riches. This hype can be directly correlated to Google searches; the more volatile the price - and regardless of whether it is high or low – the greater the increase in searches. In this way, the herd gathers its strength from the hype, which the miners use to fuel their mining.

I have a great deal of empathy for the uneducated investor who climbs into Bitcoin when the hype is at its peak, only to find volatility levels in the region of thirty to ninety percent within very short periods. There have already been at least seven similar such cycles since 2009, the most recent one being in 2017 where there was a seventy percent drop in value (from around $19 700) on 19 December 2017, to around $5 900 in January 2018.

For the uninformed, it can be emotionally exhausting and frustrating when hype turns to fear, even with Bitcoin promising to be around in years to come.

Store of Value

Bitcoin was designed to be a cost-effective and simple transaction currency and was never intended to be a 'store of value' in the manner in which it is used today.

Because the public, in general, is buying Bitcoin for the sole purpose of storing its value in order to speculate with it over time (rather than to make purchases or transact), the price of Bitcoin appreciated more than tenfold in 2017, and over 1800% by 17 December 2018. There was no correlated growth (in fact, there was actually a reduction) in the number of Bitcoin transactions, further confirming that people are not using Bitcoin for transactional purposes. Data from Coinbase (the most popular exchange in the world for buying into Bitcoin) shows that between 2013 and 2016, at least fifty percent of their users preferred to hold their Bitcoin rather than transact with it.

Bitcoin could possibly function as a 'store of value' when it is viewed as a payment transaction waiting to happen. However, as soon as it becomes speculative in nature (with people investing in crypto with a long time horizon), it disturbs the objectives of Satoshi Nakamoto and gives up its mandate as a 'store of value' in the technical sense of the meaning.

The fact that it is not being used as a transactional tool could be what brings Bitcoin (in its current format) crashing down, with the buyers drying up and the owners selling in order to make a profit, as witnessed in the December 2017 to January 2018 seventy percent price drop.

CHAPTER 8

BITCOIN: WEAKNESSES

Waiting time

I do not think there are many Bitcoin believers who would disagree that the waiting time (also known as blockwaiting) to process Bitcoin transactions is a hidden weakness in Bitcoin and a major obstacle for its use as a payment mechanism for general goods. The waiting periods to process transactions are controlled by miners who can decide which type of coins are most effective and profitable for them to mine first, and their equipment and energy resources are allocated accordingly. For the consumer, this waiting time exposes daily transactions cost to inflate, and as such, blockwaiting could be a significant deterrent to mass adoption.

The problem has been identified, and work is being done. Alternatives are always under consideration to speed up transactions and mining time, such as the hard forking of coins which allows for faster mining and higher profitability.

Litecoin was initially seen as a suitable alternative for speed and ease of transactions when compared to Bitcoin, but there has since been an avalanche of 'speed transaction coins' that have entered the market.

Transaction speeds vary substantially, and reports during March 2018 had Bitcoin averaging at 75 minutes per transaction, Bitcoin Cash at 55 minutes, Litecoin at 25 minutes, Ethereum at 8 minutes, and Ripple – one of the fastest altcoins - at 5 seconds. Only Bitshares appeared faster, at around 2 seconds per transaction.

Blockwaiting is, however, probably of little concern to the believers who prefer holding it to increase the value in their e-wallets, rather than to make purchases.

E-wallets

Many see electronic wallets (digital wallets) as a strength as they remove your money from the traditional risky exchange platforms.

Electronic wallets are supplied complete with private keys and codes and may lose their store of value if your smartphone or computer is hacked, especially if your keys and codes are stored online for safekeeping. I am of the opinion that there must be several huge electronic wallets in the system. The more their value appreciates, the more the hackers and fraudsters will go after them.

Without centralisation or any support structure for Bitcoin, the value of your electronic wallet would be worthless if you lose your private key and code. Your money will become as virtual as it gets, lost forever in a virtual world. The Bitcoins themselves would be lost from the system forever too, which could potentially decrease transaction opportunities and increase scarcity.

Any keys, passwords and codes should be recorded offline in cold storage (on paper) so as to prevent hacking. For the time being, e-wallets are a strength, until such time as they are stress tested.

```
E9873D79C6D87DC0FB6A5778633389F
4453213303DA61F20BD67FC233AA33262
```

The string of numbers above is a typical example of a private key. The one above is a hexadecimal - a numeral system made up of sixteen symbols. In the Bitcoin world, a private key is a 256-bit number, and it can be displayed in several different ways. The blockchain can make the private key as complex and as long as possible, but it is only secure as long as it cannot be discovered.

Few people would be able to memorise such a complex number, and for this reason, most people copy and save it on their computer or smartphone, something that is not recommended. Writing the key down on a piece of paper and stashing it away in a safe place would be a wiser move, especially if it is your wish that a close relative is able to find it when you pass away.

The safety of private keys has become paramount as the value of Bitcoin has escalated, so much so that a safe haven had to be found for the some of the really large e-wallets in digital space.

Such a haven was found deep in the Swiss mountains in an old decommissioned military bunker. People are able to rent private suites with customised state-of-the-art security features in order to secure their valuables. Bitcoin owners with their private keys written down on pieces of paper have become a growing customer base.

Altcoins

There has been an influx of alternative coins to Bitcoin into the market. The system is being overloaded, and the support structures are cracking under the strain of the over 1500 altcoins already in the system. There are around 180 traditional currencies in the world, but there are more than 1500 cryptocurrencies that are completely unregulated by governments or institutions.

I have been amazed at some of the names that have been coined for many of these new altcoins, including TulipToken, BananaCoin, JesusCoin, and many others. One wonders whether it is at all possible to take investing in coins with names like this seriously.

As at March 2018, Bitcoin still holds the largest market capitalisation ($194 billion). Ethereum holds second place ($85 billion), and Ripple follows in third place ($41 billion). Bitcoin's market power is growing weaker as more unique coins enter the system for mining, together with alternative methods of mining these coins with much faster transaction times.

As the number of coins increases, confusion is created in the herd and, as such, the integrity of and the trust in the system is being tested.

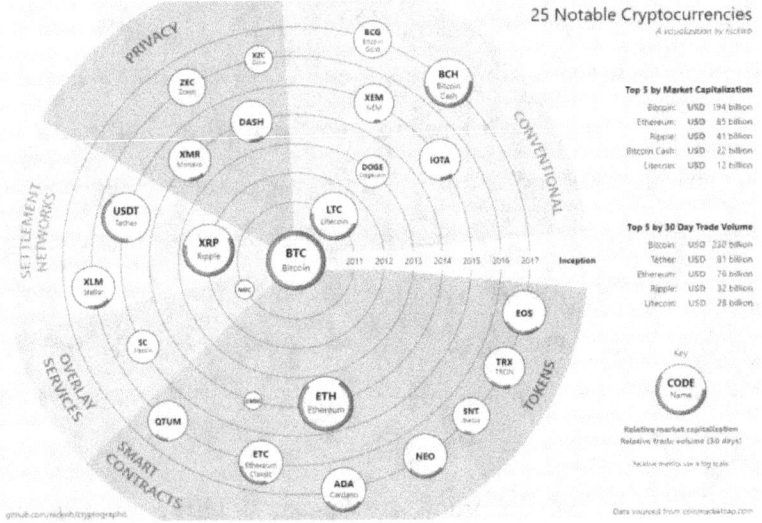

The Bloomberg diagram above clearly outlines the top 25 notable crypto coins, with Bitcoin at the core of the diagram as the 'Master Coin'. Bitcoin, as the 'master coin', could, and should, never sit on its laurels as one innovative coin could come along and remove it from its market leader pedestal. In a free market enterprise, history has proven this to be true with many products, companies, and even phenomena. The altcoins are however helping to maintain the hype around cryptocurrencies in general. There is nothing wrong with a bit of competition within the crypto ecosystem.

Kamikazes

Kamikazes were Japanese suicide pilots during the Second World War. They had one objective in mind, and that was to sink destroyers and warships.

Tim Enneking, Managing Director of Crypto Asset Management, stated that one should *"...buy the rumour and sell the news"*. Extreme volatility lures the herd towards Bitcoin as they see it as an opportunity and not a weakness. When news is positive, the going is great, but when it turns negative the going is tough! We have seen so much of this and Bitcoin's value is extremely sensitive to *any* kind of news. The most recent perfect storm of negative news could be observed between 15-20 March 2018, with ongoing regulatory news, social media advert banning, and hacking. This should never be the case if you want stability and sustainability in a currency that is being promoted to the masses.

For the skilled Bitcoin believer, this is a crucial aspect to understand because these believers prowl around such news – no matter whether it is positive or negative – because they have slick systems to overcome the bottlenecks to buy and sell quickly, thereby skimming the profits from the top.

There are many Kamikazes in the system whom I believe are willing to sacrifice everything - including the real possibilities that Bitcoin (crypto) has to offer - simply to make a quick buck, or million. This suicidal urge to drive the Bitcoin price to self-destruction through Kamikaze-induced volatility, together with the use of Bitcoin as an asset rather than a payment method for transactions as intended by the Bitcoin white paper, is by far one of the greatest weakness that Bitcoin faces.

No worth

If anyone can tell me what the real value of Bitcoin is, I will eat my hat in public, or live on LinkedIn in a recorded video. I am not aware of anyone who is willing or able to take a stab at valuing Bitcoin at present or in the future within an unregulated environment. I would even go as far as to include Satoshi Nakamoto and his anonymous cloak of secret developers in this bet.

Even if you go so far as engaging with the people who publish these hype-filled advertisements all over social media, promising that you can earn millions with crypto, they are silent on valuations. The value of Bitcoin appears to be as secretive as the creators themselves.

I find it most interesting that there is such a shroud of anonymity around Bitcoin's developers, with nobody taking public credit for its creation. Conversely, we might consider Sir Tim Berners-Lee, the creator of the World Wide Web, who did not benefit from his creation financially, but certainly took credit for creating it.

This is a mystery which requires explanation because it impacts on the long-term credibility and integrity of Bitcoin. The inherent mysterious nature of Bitcoin may lead to it becoming more of a weakness than a strength in the future.

It appears that Bitcoin is valued more as a payment platform than for its underlying blockchain technology. As I have stated previously in this book, I believe that Bitcoin is currently more of an asset class than a payment method (currency). Many believers refer to Bitcoin as an investment or an asset holding vehicle, while in reality it cannot be rationally used as an investment in a portfolio of any kind. With the possibility being strong that the bubble could burst, it bothers me that they (Satoshi Nakamoto) are making no attempt to set the original objectives back on track before their vision falls apart and dissipates before their eyes.

How much of the value is driven because of the underlying criminal and fraudulent activities using it as a medium of exchange to break the law? If criminals could be prevented from using it, how much would the value drop?

Ethereum, with its lower transaction costs, shorter settlement times and lower capacity issues, may contain more intrinsic value. Large corporates, businesses, and other entities could favour the underlying blockchain technology over Bitcoin.

Bitcoin's value is determined by the individual's perceived value of it. It has no inherent value. This is no different to fiat currency, except that fiat currencies are surrounded by regulations which, in turn, secure their value somewhat.

There is a group of people that believes the value of Bitcoin lies in the number of transactions that take place per day, although there is no clarity in terms of how this 'value' is then calculated. Some analysists have tried to predict Bitcoin prices ranging from as low as $5 000 to as high as $100 000, but to date, there has been little accuracy in terms of these predictions, and, more importantly, there have been poor track records.

The bottom line is that price and use could be significantly impacted when the believers become disillusioned. We saw this with the crisis in China (with the ban on ICOs and exchanges) as well as when institutional executives make negative statements or create rumours.

Trying to withdraw cash from a virtual platform at any time - and even more so during emotional times - is not as simple as going to an ATM around the corner. This is especially true when large amounts are involved. There are numerous built-in restrictions and time delays on coin exchanges. It is important to note that when there is a flash crash (a rapid, deep and volatile fall in prices) you may lose fifty percent or more of the value of your investment in between the time you trigger your sale mandate and when the exchange actually pays out.

The only reasonable explanation on value could be that it lies embedded within its potential to disrupt the financial and banking industry and even governments or a community of note, or it could morph into gold, an asset or a working currency.

Perhaps we should simply see crypto as part of the Fourth Industrial Revolution where value is created differently to past norms, and Bitcoin value should be viewed as a reflection of the revolution. It could be seen as the development of a new weapon of mass disruption, with Bitcoin and blockchain being the frontrunners.

Empty Promises

Wherever you look, there are people and companies promoting Bitcoin through social media, webinars, seminars, adverts and get-rich-quick YouTube videos, enticing you to enter the world of Bitcoin. Many are making outlandish predictions and promises of wealth 'beyond your wildest imagination'.

The warning bells that go along with the saying "When it sounds too good to be true, then it probably is", are clanging loudly. When everyone is telling you to buy Bitcoin "so that everyone can get wealthy together" over the next couple of years, you really should be concerned.

The promises of wealth will only materialise into actual wealth when sufficient people continue to buy in. This will allow the coins to be mined and the price to increase due to supply and demand. Sadly, as history has proved - and we appear to never learn from history - it is always the majority who enter the market right at the end, as it peaks (the dot.com bubble is a classic example), who will sacrifice their life savings, pensions, and legacy.

In December 2017, when Bitcoin spiked at just under $20 000 for one Bitcoin, the market witnessed a huge inflow of new Bitcoin buyers. This was followed by the price plummeting to below $6 000 - a typical example of such sacrifices. It is believed that up to twenty percent of these buyers made use of bad debt (credit cards, overdraft facilities, and other loans) to buy into Bitcoin, selling as the price crashed downwards in an effort to get out of it, taking the losses and additional debt with them.

Many Bitcoin believers are being fooled, and then there is the herd that is being fooled to jump on the bandwagon. Only time will tell in terms of who was right and who was wrong.

The question is whether the regulators and governments can be fooled for any extended period of time. Furthermore, will they look like fools for banning exchanges and refusing to make Bitcoin legal tender?

Can merchants be fooled to accept 'nothing' as a payment for 'something'? Or, is this one giant conspiracy and we have *all* been fooled by Satoshi Nakamoto and his cloak of secretive friends into believing the white paper that placed Bitcoin as a payment currency when it was always intended to be a speculative asset all along.

Is it possible that the creators knew that they could never be caught out as the truth would only come out one hundred years later when the last Bitcoin is mined, issued and sold, by which time they would all be dead, and it wouldn't matter?

Substantial power

Bitcoin is far from environmentally friendly. The mining of Bitcoin consumes vast quantities of energy in the form of computing power. This could make the sustainability of Bitcoin mining problematic until 2140 if alternative energy sources are not found, especially as they get closer to the twenty-one million finite coins. Perhaps Elon Musk can come up with a solution.

To put things into perspective, according to Digiconomist, to mine one Bitcoin in 2015 required enough electricity to power 1.57 American households for a day. This equates to around sixteen terawatt-hours annually. The Bitcoin network appears to be consuming energy at an annual rate of 32TWh. This is the full annual consumption of a country like Denmark. A single transaction can use around 250kWh, which equates to what an average house utilises over an eight to ten day period.

It is also believed that with the expansion of the crypto mining industry in Iceland, usage could increase to 100MW in 2018, matching the usage of its 334 000-strong population. Iceland, as mentioned previously, is prefered by many miners because of its naturally icy ambient temperatures which help to keep CPUs operating at optimal efficiency. There is also an abundance of renewable energy.

If this energy is driven by environmental unfriendly energy, then it could become problematic, even if clean energy is used. It is simply becoming too expensive to mine Bitcoin as the cryptocurrency's scarcity builds. The less Bitcoin there is to mine, the more complex the mining process will become, and the more supercomputers will be required.

The consumption problem has been highlighted as recently as March 2018, when the New York State Public Services Commission (PSC) agreed that municipal power companies can now add a surcharge to Bitcoin miners who benefit from the state's abundance of cheap hydroelectric power. Imagine if China, where at least eighty percent of the largest Bitcoin 'mining pools' are based, picks up on this and bills a surcharge to their massively cost-effective hydro plants. This could have a negative impact on the profitability of creating Bitcoins.

It is clear that the profitability of Bitcoin mining is directly linked to the price of Bitcoin; the higher the price, the more profitable it is to mine, and vice versa. There is a breakeven point where mining is simply not viable, and this tends to differ vastly depending on where in the world the mining is taking place. In Iceland, the breakeven point would be at a much lower level than in India or South Africa where the temperatures are warmer and coal – abundantly available – is used as the primary energy source.

A March 2018 Fundstrat report reported an average cost of $8 038 to mine a single Bitcoin. This figure is based on a mining model that was set up by their science team that incorporates the cost of equipment, electricity, cooling facilities, and general overheads, inclusive of labour. If one considers that the average price of Bitcoin during March 2018 was in the region of $8 000, with a range of between $7 400 and $9 500, it is evident that the cost of mining is at a critical point. When the cost to mine Bitcoin exceeds its rewards, miners lose their incentive to keep mining. Some might simply switch their expensive equipment off during these periods or mine a more profitable coin, while hoping for the price to return above the breakeven point. This point will continue to escalate with equipment maintenance and replacement becoming increasingly more expensive. With a depressed price range in early 2018, and a possibly bleak outlook for the remainder of 2018, the profitability odds are stacking up against the miners.

Security

Bitcoin security can be both a strength and a weakness. There are numerous security issues that surround Bitcoin, such as the Bitcoin electronic wallet (with or without cold storage), the latest double password security application available on certain smartphones, and the fact that exchanges are being regularly hacked these days. Bitcoin holders who store their Bitcoins on the exchange platforms (rather than off-site in electronic wallets) are at great risk. In South Africa, for example, when purchasing Bitcoin through an exchange like Luno, it is recommended that buyers immediately transfer their coins to an e-wallet. An e-wallet cannot be hacked, unless the hacker is able to get their hands on your private key (much in the same way as the PIN for your ATM card).

The word 'Crypto' elicits connotations of strong built-in security, but Bitcoin has, unfortunately, proven to be extremely easy to steal from an exchange, and even easier to lose once your private code is lost. Hacking has been made easier with the two-step authentication system that uses cell phone numbers to access emails and virtual money accounts. Once the hackers have control of the phone number, they have a backdoor through which to hack your e-wallet. What should have been a strength has become a bit of a weakness to some users.

The North Korean hackers who attempted to steal Bitcoins from South Korea between May 2017 and July 2017 (as confirmed by FireEye) were a wakeup call for the industry. Questions have been raised over whether ISIS and other terrorist groups are using Bitcoin (along with other criminals) for money laundering and criminal activities.

Security concerns can come from many sources. Even miners risk exposure, as was seen recently in Iceland with six hundred mining computers (worth in the region of $2 000 000) being stolen. However, the value within these computers could be worth billions of Dollars. This was grand theft on a scale that has, up until now, never been seen, and was clearly the work of a well-organised crime syndicate.

Estates

As a TEP® and CFP®, it is important for me to make mention of this.

What happens to your Bitcoin account when you pass away?

This really depends on whether you have taken care of your estate planning and made certain that your executor has clear instructions together with having access to all your passwords and private codes. It is, however, also an opportunity for unscrupulous executors to abuse their fiduciary duties, or a greedy family member – who does not know better – staking a claim to your Bitcoin account.

Ownership of Bitcoins is associated with an address and a digital sign-in with a private key. Without knowledge of the key, transactions are simply not possible. If the key is lost at any time, and especially upon death, the Bitcoin network will not recognise any proof of ownership, and especially not letters from executors or powers of attorney.

Bitcoin is pseudonymous, meaning that funds are not tied to real-world entities but, instead, to unidentifiable addresses.

Bitcoin, like social media and application intellectual property, brings a new dimension to estates and estate planning. Could Bitcoin die a slow death with its owner if ownership is not regularly transferred?

One major problem would be estate liquidity if the Bitcoin e-wallet in question is, for instance, mostly made up of Bitcoins purchased between 2009 and end 2016, before the over 1000% climb since January 2017.

The problem surrounds the tax impact on profits and the value of the estate inclusive of Bitcoins. In South Africa, this is referred to as capital gains tax (CGT) and estate duty tax.

An e-wallet could boost the liquidation and distribution account to well above the R 3 500 000 allowable 4A abatement (in terms of the Estate Duty Act, Act 45 of 1955) and chase up the 20% estate duty for estates under R 30 000 000 in value, and 25% for estates above this threshold. The capital gain on these older e-wallets (since 2009) could be enormous, severely impacting on estate liquidity if these coins cannot be sold on the open market within a short space of time while the estate is being wound up. This is made worse if the estate planner did not allow for a life cover policy to cover estate taxes or to ensure estate liquidity.

Financial advisors and estate planners should be making this a serious discussion point during their annual reviews with clients who are crypto owners.

Switching

In a virtual world like Bitcoin the word 'cash' is heavily frowned upon (and probably a swear word more than anything else). Virtual currency's only purpose should be for the payment of goods and commodities, or for money transfers and similar transactions.

People might look at you as if you are from another planet if you start asking questions about how to switch between virtual cash (Bitcoin) and hard cash (fiat), especially when the price of Bitcoin is escalating and you want to take profits, or cash in your millions.

This was one of my initial questions, and there was little available reading material on the subject at the time, until I discovered this invaluable article on selling Bitcoin on

CoinDesk's website at www.coindesk.com/information/sell-Bitcoin

As the article explains, Bitcoin was not designed to be cashed out easily because its sole purpose was supposed to be for the exchange for goods. Buying goods is not a priority for Bitcoin owners; instead, it is about cashing in on profits. There are simply not enough merchants approving the use of Bitcoin as a form of tender. The number of merchants is actually reducing. This is due to Bitcoin's volatility which does not work well with the financials of a merchant from an accounting perspective.

The real stories of Bitcoin owners wanting to cash out and who have followed the cumbersome process of switching between wallets, platforms, exchanges or peer-to-peer, and who end up with a computer screen flashing the words *'operational error'*, only to see their money pay out three months later, can be found everywhere. The stories are even worse with many of the altcoins.

Do not expect to receive a single payment when cashing out larger amounts (for example $1 000 000). You will likely receive several batch payments which will take place only when Bitcoin 'buyers' are prepared to buy into the Bitcoin you have up for sale for a price that *they* are willing to pay.

This is even more difficult during a Bitcoin bull run, with most 'hodlers' refusing to buy at higher prices. In terms of cryptocurrencies, the concept of a willing buyer and willing seller takes on a whole new meaning when it comes to price and value perceptions.

CHAPTER 9

BITCOIN: OPPORTUNITIES

Optimism

People are generally optimistic in nature and want to believe that life will present favourable opportunities, and, if a 'regular' opportunity does not come along, then they peg their hopes on luck playing a role. This is most certainly the case when something like Bitcoin comes along with its tempting promises to 'get rich quick', and even more so when it is open to the population as a whole. With opportunities knocking on your smartphone through social media and the like, it is difficult to resist when everybody else is jumping on the bandwagon. Bitcoin requires mass adoption in order to sustain its upward momentum and to maintain its existence. The price may stabilise one day when it becomes more regulated, but, for now, opportunity is breaking down the doors, and it can be difficult to ignore it or make sense of it.

Phenomenon

If we analyse price charts from the past five years, it would be fair to say that Bitcoin could be perceived as a massive success story for the early adopters. Bitcoin (and its 'digital asset' crypto friends), supported by ongoing good news stories, and with social media functioning as a *virtual steroid booster*, has become a global phenomenon today.

The Bitcoin price is most certainly a *phenomenon* when one plots its movement on the charts. With it reaching new record highs in December 2017, followed by its subsequent major downward correction in January 2018, and then doubling up since its lowest correction point, it appears to be a speculative asset for the time being, with its volatile ups and downs having become the norm. This is not a strong foundation on which to support any form of valuation because one would be riding on what can only be seen as a phenomenon, rather than something with real intrinsic value and potential.

Payment tool

Bitcoin was designed to operate as both a medium of exchange and a method of payment, with cryptography technology being its main driver and management tool.

The problem is most people are using it as a speculative investment and not as electronic cash to pay for goods and services. Price opportunity is overriding its originally intended use, and there are limited merchants who accept Bitcoin as a method of payment, with some of them (of late) even walking away from it due to the volatility of the price during transactions.

The process with which one can make payment with Bitcoin is cumbersome. Who would in their right mind would want to purchases goods with Bitcoin when it means potentially losing out on an opportunity to make massive profits by holding onto it? With the convenience of fiat money at your disposal, why would you even go through the cumbersome Bitcoin transaction process to buy a McDonald's burger when your meal will be cold before the transaction is approved, leaving you with nothing but exorbitantly high transaction fees to contend with, and a poor taste in your mouth?

Statistics are certainly not reflecting Bitcoin's popularity as a payment method on websites who accept such coins. This is because people who are buying coins are investors and not shoppers. The lack of transactional activity is driving price – in the same way as gold has performed throughout history –

despite the fact that Bitcoin has no industrial value, unlike gold.

Unfortunately, these practices are hampering the core design of Bitcoin as a payment or currency tool. This is where an opportunity can become a weakness. There may, however, be some good news on the horizon with Singapore' Central Bank's 'Project Ubin'. The bank is in the process of developing three new blockchain prototypes to incorporate interbank payments and settlements with digital tokens. These tokens would represent the Singapore Dollar as a digital entity, and could, therefore, be used for decentralised interbank payments and settlements with liquidity savings mechanisms.

A major opportunity for Bitcoin would be if a company like Amazon, or even Alibaba (if China changes their mind on Bitcoin, or issues their own cryptocurrency) accepts Bitcoin as a means of payment. Major brand acceptance on this level would be embraced by the masses and could be the critical breakthrough point required by Bitcoin in order to go mainstream in the future, if it survives the bubble, of course.

Oasis of wealth

2017 will become known as the 'Bitcoin coming-of-age year', with little getting in the way of stopping its volatility. It certainly does not seem to matter if its price is driven by mass *payment* adoption or mass *asset* adoption. What people are really adopting is the 'oasis of wealth' which is being proclaimed (with or without misrepresentation) through social and other media.

Returns

When the return on an investment far exceeds the norms of any return generated in the past four hundred years, it is no wonder that the herd is flocking towards Bitcoin. With returns at 1800% at one stage towards the end of December 2017 (before the correction after 19 December 2017) - no matter how unrealistic such gains are in the greater scheme of things, not to mention its inherent volatility - it is difficult for the herd to ignore.

With Bitcoin not even making the top ten for returns in cryptocurrencies in 2017 (according to CoinDesk statistics), it is easy to appreciate the current hype around altcoins which are yielding significantly higher returns. Bitcoin came in at number fourteen, with Ripple at number one (36 000% growth), and OmisaGO at number ten (3315% growth).

Forbes named Bitcoin the *best* investment of the year for 2013, and Bloomberg named Bitcoin the *worst* investment of 2014. It is notable how your fortunes can turn. I wonder who will be the first to name Bitcoin the 'best investment' for 2017. If one were to speak in technical investment terms, Bitcoin would not only be the best investment for 2017, but the best investment since the term *investment* was 'coined' centuries ago.

When one considers that Bitcoin was the first cryptocurrency to enter the market (even after forking) and its resilient performance and resistance to bad news, not to mention its real potential as a cryptocurrency (rather than an asset class), I would give it a somewhat better chance of success than any of the other 1500+ cryptocurrencies currently in the market. I would, however, give Ethereum a strong bet because of its flexibility and the future potential created by the unique underlying blockchain applications that it has at its disposal.

What will 2018 bring for Bitcoin investors? Even after the January 2018 crash, there are predictions of $50 000 to $100 000 for one Bitcoin by the end of 2018, and a combined market value for crypto sitting at over $1 trillion. Optimistic or not? I strongly doubt the reliability of such a prediction which, in all likelihood is simply more hype from the evangelists.

Returning to its record high of close to $20 000 would already be a great achievement, before the other levels even come into consideration. Until the $13 000 threshold is sustained for at least thirty days, any higher predictions can be placed on the back burner. The question should rather be around *how low* Bitcoin can go in 2018. I am of the opinion that once the $8 000 level becomes unsustainable, with $6 000 being breached on the down, that a low of around $3 000 may not be entirely impossible (for a short period), before the buy-in at such levels pushes it back upwards and its resilience kicks in (as we have seen many times). The alternative is the bubble simply bursting because of fear selling; something which would cause major liquidity problems on exchanges worldwide, to the point of seeing them completely shut down[4].

Talk it up

Beyond the power of word of mouth is *the word of social media*. The immediate impact on the price of Bitcoin is clearly visible as soon as people start talking Bitcoin up. The same effect comes into play when people start talking it down.

Bitcoin's price does not reflect the use of crypto as a form of currency at all; it simply reflects its speculative value created

---

[4] *As I have stated on the first page of this book, this is not advice but simply scenarios that come to mind, and should not be used to go short or long on Bitcoin at any stage.*

by an emotional opportunity that has been waved in front of unsuspecting investors.

With celebrities like Paris Hilton, Jamie Foxx, Floyd Mayweather – and even icons like Bill Gates and Richard Branson – all talking about Bitcoin and the blockchain (although, in my opinion, their support lies with the blockchain more than with crypto), Bitcoin appears to have a positive outlook. With Michele Mone, the Bra Baroness, advertising her exclusive offer to Bitcoin believers to buy into a property development in Dubai, people are now in a position to see real value coming from their Bitcoins through asset conversions.

Similarly, when senior executives and institutions in the financial sector (like Goldman Sachs, who recently announced that they will form trading operations dedicated to Bitcoin and digital currencies) start speaking positively about Bitcoin, then interest and awareness propels ongoing positive momentum and neutralises negative comments made by people like Jamie Dimon.

Morgan Stanley's CEO, James Gorman, was quoted as saying, "The concept of anonymous currency is an interesting one because of the privacy protection it affords people, as well as what it says to the central banking systems about controlling it."

When governments and regulatory bodies, like those in Japan, not only talking Bitcoin up, but also granting licences to eleven exchanges to operate, it certainly impacts positively on cryptocurrency, opening up further opportunities.

Japan has, in fact, become the most Bitcoin-friendly and efficient place of business for crypto and its investors in the world. If Ethereum were to follow suit, this would bode well for cryptocurrencies and the blockchain in general. Malaysia has legalised Bitcoin as an industry as well as the use of digital currency. Countries like Russia, Philippines, Thailand, Vietnam, Switzerland and Singapore are all seriously considering regulating the Bitcoin and blockchain industry in one way or another.

Unite against the norm

2009 was the perfect time to launch Bitcoin. With many people completely disillusioned after the subprime crisis of 2008, many people were anti-government and anti-establishment. People were horrified that the banks were being bailed out with their hard-earned tax money. These banks had committed "crimes", yet nobody was going to jail.

This perfect storm gave Bitcoin a unique opportunity to enter the marketplace.

Bitcoin 'investors' are being sold on the fact that government-issued currencies cannot be trusted, and that Bitcoin is the future of money. Many Bitcoin believers – post-2008 – are referring to Bitcoin as a 'gift from God' to help humanity clean up the mess caused by the banks during the subprime crisis. Unfortunately, if the Bitcoin phenomenon had to come crashing down there would be no protection for its investors, with no government, bank or other institution backing Bitcoin in its current unregulated ecosystem.

Niche

Bitcoin could be perceived as owning its niche in the cryptocurrency industry, supported by its underlying blockchain technology. It is this niche that could protect it against the altcoin stampede within the Bitcoin domain. Its finite twenty-one million coins also place it in a 'scarcity' niche. This is a highly debatable point, and I will come back to it later.

Integrity

Cryptocurrency hedge funds like BlockTower Capital, launched in August 2017, and who hired Matthew Goetz, a former Goldman Sachs vice president, to spearhead the company, quickly lends integrity to Bitcoin. Goldman Sachs themselves have committed to Bitcoin, cryptocurrencies and blockchain which shows strong support towards the industry. The beginning of futures in the USA and Australia certainly help to build credibility and integrity.

Mike Novogratz, billionaire and ex-fund manager of Fortress Investment Group (and also a former Goldman Sachs partner), has returned to the hedge fund industry, proclaiming to wanting to be the 'King of Bitcoin'. He has unveiled the launch of Galaxy Digital, a cryptocurrency 'merchant bank' with 'full service, digital assets'. It is described by some as the 'Goldman Sachs for Crypto', with the idea being to raise over $200 million in capital. Galaxy Digital would bring a new dimension to the price of crypto and possibly even its life expectancy. As somebody who has lost fortunes, Novogratz sees the major fortunes made and lost within crypto as an excellent reason to come back into major capital investment markets and take advantage of the old 'fear and greed' investment principle.

Hedge funds like Polychain Capital and MetaStable Capital, who operate within a broader mandate, trading in equities, bonds and other capital investments (but include crypto) add significant integrity to Bitcoin's reputation, boosting opportunities for crypto sales and price escalations.

Trust

Goldman Sachs recently referred to a study which labelled the blockchain as 'the new technology of trust'. With the blockchain being the underlying platform for Bitcoin, the believers and herd inherently trust the cryptocurrency. Goldman Sachs' endorsement and commitment to Bitcoin will most certainly aid in these trust factors.

Independence

The triumph of Bitcoin is that it cuts out the middleman, referring to itself as a peer-to-peer electronic cash system, giving the system independence from third party involvement and interference, thereby preventing additional cost and fees. I am of the opinion that the miners are the 'middlemen', seeing as they are replacing the intermediaries (or bankers) and are paid in Bitcoins, over and above the transaction fees that they may charge to speed up validations. They are required to timestamp each transaction, and to only include the transaction that comes first, thereby preventing double payments on any single transaction[5]. If the miners can maintain their independence without manipulating the mining process, crypto pricing, and hard-forking, then it will bring

---

[5] *The risk of double payments (with digital currencies) was taken care of through the creation of the blockchain.*

positive long-term opportunities to Bitcoin. The current trends are, however, proving quite the opposite.

Exchanges and e-wallets

The exchanges play a critical role in the success of mass Bitcoin adoption. Many exchanges are under threat from governments and regulators due to concerns over fraud and security, and the masses need to feel confident about transacting on them.

Exchanges with tight security, and especially those that use multi-signature security will drive further buy-in by untapped sections of the market. New investors should ideally be educated to use exchanges as little as possible, and certainly not as crypto storage platforms.

- **How do exchanges and e-wallets work?**

Peer-to-peer' (P2P) or 'decentralised' exchanges are operated and maintained exclusively by software. Exchanges allow Peer-to-Peer participants to trade without a trusted third party.

Crypto exchanges work exclusively with pre-programmed software, with no input from any human middlemen. It is a decentralised, fully-automated system that operates based on the buyer's terms.

The exchange software is capable of matching traders with each other in a decentralised manner. Exchanges match peer-to-peer orders to the people behind each order. When a matching buy-and-sell order is found, the exchange connects the buyer with the seller, thereby allowing them (by default) to close the deal without any intermediaries.

In order not to become a victim of hacking or fraud, experts recommend that you do not keep any money floating around in the cloud on an exchange. This is where e-wallets come in. Crypto users must have a digital wallet to store and transact with digital currencies of all kinds, including ICO tokens.

Digital wallets have significant advantages over our old fiat wallets because everything is electronic and at your fingertips. E-wallets are basically digital applications with sophisticated, flexible features with the ability to fully record all transactions. They allow you to immediately move your digital money between exchanges without keeping it on an exchange.

E-wallets can be created via a web browser or downloaded onto your smartphone. E-wallets work with a unique digital key, commonly known as a *private key* or a *master key*, made up of hexadecimal codes and consisting of a long sequence of numbers and letters which are virtually impossible to memorise. These keys should be written down and saved and certainly not saved in any digital format due to the possibility of hacking. Your private key should never be shared, and it should be stored safely in a location from where it can be retrieved. You should, however, leave information in terms of where it can be found if you happen to pass away.

The recent massive cryptocurrency exchange hack of Japan's Tokyo-based Coincheck in January 2018 (300 000 XEM altcoin tokens), has brought to the fore the vulnerability of crypto exchanges. With the extent of the hack reaching around $500 million + in digital money, it far supersedes the $450 million Mt. Gox hack in 2014. At the time of the hack, Mt. Gox handled eighty percent of the world's Bitcoin trades.

As recently as March 2018, hackers again caused 'irregular trades' at Binance, by far one of the largest exchanges in the world. Hacks like this are happening more often than not with exchanges operating in legal grey zones. Binance blamed a large scale phishing and stealing attempt, and assured clients that all funds were safe. They were, however, unable to reverse some of the trades that were targeted. It has become critical for crypto owners to secure their account credentials.

Scarcity

Bitcoin's greatest opportunity is probably its unique scarcity model. With a 'finite' number of only 21 million Bitcoins (in theory) available, and currently over 16.8 million issued Bitcoins in circulation (leaving under five million remaining), the scarcity is building. Additional scarcity is building with every Bitcoin that is *lost* in the system.

Bitcoin is creating 'artificial scarcity' in the same way as it is created for fine art. It will have value for as long as people believe that it *has* value, and for that, a willing buyer and seller is the only requirement.

As the twenty-one million mark approaches, the mining rewards (currently paid to the miners in Bitcoins) will be phased out, making the cost to mine Bitcoins higher than what the rewards are worth. This could result in commissions, fees (or similar) being paid to the miners instead, which will obviously negatively impact on transaction fees. My concern is that once this point is reached in 2140 when the last Bitcoin is mined, the fees alone would not be sufficient enough to incentivise the miners to keep on mining. To increase the fees to make up for the loss of Bitcoin remuneration, would make day to day transaction cost to expensive and could simply spell the end of Bitcoin as a transaction tool forever.

This will become unchartered territory when the halving ceases in time, with transactions fees becoming exorbitant

This could lead to a syndicate of miners setting rates and reducing Bitcoin's opportunities. Another (possibly far-fetched) scenario could be the miners deciding that, in order to keep the ecosystem going and in an effort to prevent the mining industry (and hence Bitcoin itself) from collapsing, that they would use their own Bitcoins to facilitate ongoing transactions, and accept lower fees for validating these transactions.

The issue of *limited coins* is most interesting. They may be limited in issue by Bitcoin, but this fact completely ignores the growing number of altcoins coming into play. While the supply of Bitcoins is limited, the supply of virtual currency is *unlimited*. The existence of these altcoins reduces the scarcity impact. This would become more apparent if some of these altcoins proved to offer high levels of integrity, trust, more cost-effective transaction costs, and more efficient mining methods than Bitcoin currently offers.

Bitcoins can also be subdivided through a process known as *hard forking*. A hard fork takes place when a single cryptocurrency is split in half. This is something that can take place across all cryptocurrencies. During a hard fork, the developers create a software update for a particular cryptocurrency, and all coins are required to update to the latest version. The hard fork creates an old version of a coin and a new version (and also a new blockchain), and the holder of that particular cryptocurrency will receive one new coin for every old one that they own.

Bitcoin experienced its first hard fork in August 2017. A hard fork can only take place when there is consensus among 92% of the miners, which is a difficult number to reach in practice. The question remains in terms of how further hard forks would impact on Bitcoin's 'finite' number of coins? Even though Bitcoin was the first coin on the market (making it a trusted brand), I don't believe that Bitcoin (and Satoshi for that matter) would have wanted to be a part of this process of hard forking. At this stage, to obtain a 50% consensus would be miraculous on its own.

For those interested in the concept of splitting or hard forking within Bitcoin and why some say "yes" and some say "no", I have included an article (with approval) that was posted on Bitcoin Magazine's website in October 2017 at the end of this chapter.

The Bitcoin blockchain has forked several times since August 2017, but future forks are widely expected to be tumultuous, leading to increased confusion over which version of Bitcoin is the 'real' version. I expect at least one or two forks in 2018.

Are the miners actually planning on 'firing' Bitcoin 1.0?

Based on current calculations, the last of the twenty-one million coins will only be mined around 2140, but this might change when one considers factors such as artificial intelligence, changes to technology, and alternative power breakthroughs that could power computers in ways beyond our current understanding.

Bitcoin protocols could be changed at any time to allow more Bitcoins to enter the market. One does have to wonder how it is possible that over sixteen million coins have been mined since 2009 (to date), but yet it would take another one hundred years to mine the remaining less than five million coins. Wikipedia explains the halving protocol as follows:

> *"Supply Growth: 12.5 Bitcoins per block (every 10 minutes) until mid-2020 (possibly 6 June), and then afterwards 6.25 Bitcoins per block for 4 years until next halving. This halving then continues until 2140 when 21 million Bitcoins will have been issued."*

Why would the secretive developers have come up with a system that would slow the mining process down so drastically, essentially over a human lifetime, given today's current high rates of life expectancy? Could it perhaps (as I have eluded to before) have something to do with creating an illusion of long-term scarcity to support a growing demand, combined with a high escalation in prices due to Bitcoin's apparent short supply?

Many believers are stating that Bitcoin is 'deflationary' in nature (because, unlike fiat currency, there will come a time when no new Bitcoins are 'printed') but the alternative could be argued that it is 'inflationary' as a result of alternative Bitcoins (such as Bitcoin Cash), as well as through future forking.

Bitcoin remains the *hot* coin, but when you start comparing it to Ethereum, Ripple and Litecoin (and other better-known altcoins with their better capabilities and growth), it can rather be seen as *lukewarm*, as reflected in its reducing market share.

The reason I believe Bitcoin is currently staying ahead of the growing pack of altcoins is its market cap of forty-two percent. It is currently still in the lead based on volume, but it was already decreasing while I was writing this book. I believe that it could drop as low as 30% to 35% in the year that lies ahead.

This is the unedited article from Bitcoin Magazine at I referred to earlier. For the technically-minded folk out there, enjoy the read.

2x or NO2X: Why Some Want to Hard Fork Bitcoin — and Why Others Do Not

By: Aaron van Wirdum

Bitcoin Magazine, 6 October 2017

Source: https://Bitcoinmagazine.com/articles/2x-or-no2x-why-some-want-hard-fork-Bitcoin-november-and-why-others-dont/

A group of Bitcoin companies plans to deploy a hard fork to double Bitcoin's block weight limit to eight megabytes this November. Known as 'SegWit2x,' this incompatible protocol change follows from the New York Agreement (NYA) and is embedded in the BTC1 software client.

SegWit2x is highly controversial. Most of Bitcoin's development community, a number of other companies, some mining pools and — if public polls and futures markets are representative — a majority of users and the market are not on board with this hard fork. Some of them are even engaged in a sort of protest movement, under the banner 'NO2X.'

For those who have not kept up with the debate, here's an overview of the main arguments for and against the 2x hard fork part of SegWit2x.

Author's note: Of course, not all proponents of SegWit2x agree with all of the arguments in favor of the hard fork, and not all opponents agree with all of the arguments against it. This is just a general (and probably incomplete) overview of the various arguments out there.

YES to lower transaction fees and/or faster confirmations

Many proponents of a block size limit increase believe that one of Bitcoin's main value propositions is its potential as a payment rail. They prefer on-chain transactions to be cheaper and faster than they have been recently, and think this is what the silent majority of users wants as well. SegWit2x proponents are often also a bit more willing to risk Bitcoin's other defining features, such as censorship resistance.

With bigger Bitcoin blocks, the network can handle more transactions. This should drive average fees down and have transactions confirm faster. Or it should at least make it more expensive for attackers to spam the network with bogus transactions, if they do try to drive fees and confirmation times up. SegWit2x proponents therefore think that a hard fork to double Bitcoin's block weight limit will onboard more users more quickly.

Faster adoption could, in turn, benefit Bitcoin in several ways. Bitcoin's exchange rate could increase, which would also grow miner revenue, which should translate to more hash power to secure the network.

Meanwhile, more total users may run full nodes to benefit geographic network decentralization. Furthermore, increased popularity might even make it harder for governments to ban Bitcoin.

YES to compromising

The New York Agreement was born in the heat of Bitcoin's scaling debate under the looming threat of a contentious hard fork led by the alternative protocol implementation Bitcoin Unlimited. This effort was, to a large extent, spearheaded by proponents of a block size limit increase and opponents of the Segregated Witness (SegWit) protocol upgrade, like Bitmain and Bitcoin.com.

These companies leveraged hash power from their mining pools to delay SegWit activation, while planning to increase the block size limit with a hard fork. This could have "split" the Bitcoin network into two incompatible blockchains and currencies.

SegWit2x was presented as a middle-of-the-road compromise between the two warring camps of the scaling debate. "One side" would get SegWit, while the "other side" would get a capacity increase hard

fork. Most signatories believed, at least at the time of the agreement, that this would be a solution that should keep the Bitcoin network together.

YES to keeping their word

While doubling Bitcoin's block size would (probably) decrease average fees and/or confirmation times, the recent activation of SegWit did already decrease both quite a bit. What may, therefore, be more important for remaining signatories of the NYA is not so much the block weight increase but rather the agreement in and of itself. Dropping out of the agreement "halfway" — after SegWit activation but before the hard fork — would be a breach of the agreement they signed on to.

Not only that, but dropping out now could also be seen as an admission that SegWit was actually not so much activated because of the NYA in the first place — but rather because of the BIP 148 user-activated soft fork (UASF). Due to BIP 148's controversial nature, not in the least among some of the

NYA signatories, many may be eager to avoid the perception that this UASF was a success.

YES to "firing" Bitcoin Core

Currently, most people running full nodes choose to use a Bitcoin Core software client, making this the dominant implementation on the Bitcoin network. Some even consider it Bitcoin's protocol-defining "reference client."

SegWit2x appears to be at least partially motivated by the desire to remove the perceived power or influence that Bitcoin Core contributors have over Bitcoin's protocol development, by having a majority of companies and miners switch to the BTC1 software client instead. (It should be noted that within this context, "firing" actually means "no longer using software maintained by these developers." Bitcoin Core contributors are essentially volunteers and cannot literally be fired, while most of the code in the BTC1 client is forked from Bitcoin Core and thus written by Bitcoin Core developers anyway.)

Bitcoin Core contributors could, of course, release a new Bitcoin Core client that adopts the SegWit2x hard fork to make it compatible with BTC1, and therefore compatible with these companies and miners. In fact, this might even be what many NYA signatories are hoping for. In that case

BTC1 would effectively become Bitcoin's new reference client, at least from the perspective of some of these signatories.

Other signatories may prefer the Bitcoin Core development team to quit altogether. In some cases, support for the hard fork may even be largely driven by resentment toward the Bitcoin Core project and a desire to take any action perceived to discredit it.

YES to miners being the deciding factor

Over 90 percent of miners (by hash power) are currently signaling support for SegWit2x. While this signaling itself is technically meaningless, SegWit2x proponents assume that miners will follow through on this stated intent.

Some SegWit2x proponents argue that miners decide the future of the Bitcoin protocol — or that miners should decide. If a hard fork were to result in two incompatible blockchains, they believe that whichever blockchain has more hash power dedicated to it is the "real" Bitcoin. Or, at least, they'll maintain that the blockchain with the most hash power dedicated to it will be the more secure and functional "Bitcoin," and thus the "Bitcoin" that people will want to use.

NO to more security tradeoffs

SegWit2x opponents generally agree that increasing Bitcoin's block size comes with a number of tradeoffs.

For one, bigger blocks increase resource requirements for operating a full node, such as more bandwidth use, longer sync time for new nodes and more. This increases the cost for individual users to partake in the network in a trustless and therefore optimally secure manner. This increased cost could, in turn, have a centralizing effect on the network, especially if it results in fewer users running full nodes.

Additionally, bigger blocks would slow down block propagation over the peer-to-peer network, which potentially benefits larger miners and mining pools: another centralizing effect.

And it may actually be good to limit network throughput to some extent, as this increases fee pressure, which in turn provides an incentive for miners to secure the network as block rewards dwindle over time.

All these types of risks can ultimately lead to a more centralized and therefore less censorship-resistant and less permissionless Bitcoin. This is sometimes referred to as the "PayPal 2.0 risk," where Bitcoin degrades to lose what

SegWit2x opponents consider to be its defining features and main value propositions. With the activation of Segregated Witness, Bitcoin allows for a worst case of four-megabyte blocks, increased from one megabyte. Some consider this to be a somewhat risky compromise already. SegWit2x would double this risk to a worst-case total of eight megabytes, which SegWit2x opponents generally consider too big for now.

NO to "backroom deals"

While the details are a bit unclear (and that is part of the problem), SegWit2x was forged between a relatively small group of (mostly) executives from prominent Bitcoin companies during an invite-only meeting in a hotel in New York, organized by the Digital Currency Group.

After agreeing on what they considered to be a compromise between the two sides of the scaling debate, they reached out to other companies to sign on to the agreement. The aggregate customer base of all these signatories is claimed to be represented by the agreement, as is all hash power connected to participating mining pools.

Further, while BTC1 technically has an open development mailing list and an open Slack discussion channel (though both were initially closed), not much discussion is taking place in either of these venues. This either means that not much development discussion is taking place at all — or that these discussions are taking place within an unknown closed environment, too.

All this is in stark contrast with the open-source ethos in which Bitcoin was born and which still permeates Bitcoin's development process today. Bitcoin Core contributors, for example, meet and discuss publicly on IRC, while potential protocol changes (BIPs) are discussed on a public mailing list; both communication channels are relatively active.

Moreover, SegWit2x opponents typically consider it a key feature of Bitcoin that users are in control of their own money. While companies may provide services, SegWit2x opponents don't think these companies should get to decide what defines Bitcoin on behalf of their customers and should definitely not make them on behalf of all Bitcoin users.

All this is not just a matter of principle: opponents believe SegWit2x could actually set a bad precedent. If a small group of companies is shown to be effectively in control of the Bitcoin protocol, these companies could become a sort of central point of failure. Governments could, for example, exert pressure on them to introduce black lists or other infringements on (what they consider to be) Bitcoin's core features.

NO to "firing" Bitcoin Core

While Bitcoin Core is indeed the dominant client on the Bitcoin network, this is only because users voluntarily choose to run this software — and many SegWit2x opponents, at least, are happy to do so.

They have no desire to "fire" the Bitcoin Core development team at all.

It's also not clear if any group of developers can or will take the place of Bitcoin Core's current contributors should they be "fired." Not many people in the world have as deep an understanding of Bitcoin's codebase or inner workings as they do.

BTC1, for example, really has only one developer doing most of the work on it: Bloq CEO Jeff Garzik. Garzik does have experience working on the Bitcoin Core codebase, but his core experience is not in working on consensus-critical code. This also means that testing and review of BTC1 is rather minimal.

And while some SegWit2x proponents hope and believe that Bitcoin Core developers will merge the SegWit2x code or otherwise shift their efforts to the SegWit2x version of Bitcoin after the hard fork, this seems very unlikely: the project went so far as to issue a rare joint statement rejecting SegWit2x. Instead, if the SegWit2x hard fork were to succeed and the current Bitcoin protocol were to stop functioning, several Bitcoin Core developers have indicated they'd consider that outcome to represent a failure of Bitcoin itself and would choose to move on to different projects altogether.

Lastly, it should be noted that — while dominant — Bitcoin Core is not the only software client that embeds the current Bitcoin protocol. Bitcoin Knots, Libbitcoin, Bcoin and a range of other alternative implementations do so as well. SegWit2x would arguably be "firing" not just Bitcoin Core but most of the entire development community.

NO to contentious hard forks

Since not everyone agrees that the SegWit2x hard fork is the best way forward, or even beneficial at all, it is contentious. And many SegWit2x critics oppose any contentious hard fork for two main reasons.

The first reason is philosophical. SegWit2x opponents think that Bitcoin's gold-like resistance to change is one of its key value propositions. More specifically, they maintain that the rules of the system should not be changed against a user's will: that would undermine trust in this type of money.

The second reason is similar, but more technical: not only shouldn't the rules be changed against a user's will, the rules cannot be changed against a user's will. As long as users run full nodes and do not switch to SegWit2x, the original Bitcoin protocol will continue to exist. As such, a hard fork like SegWit2x won't actually change the existing Bitcoin at all; rather, it would create a new blockchain and a new currency — a coin-split.

This also explains why SegWit2x is not considered a "compromise" by opponents. For them, the SegWit2x hard fork is not a middle-in-the-middle compromise. Instead, such a contentious hard fork is precisely the thing they do not want.

NO to rushed hard forks

Even if the hard fork was not contentious, SegWit2x opponents would consider it rushed. Since everyone needs to upgrade for a hard fork to be successful — that is, there is no resulting coin-split — many think that typical hard forks should require a year of lead time at the very least, and maybe even two years or longer.

SegWit2x had a lead time of three months since SegWit activation and about six months since the agreement was made. Opponents consider this recklessly short even for popular hard forks — never mind contentious ones.

NO to a lack of replay protection

If SegWit2x does lead to a coin-split — and the current lack of consensus suggests that it will — there would be two blockchains and coins with a shared history: one coin that follows the current Bitcoin protocol and one coin that follows the SegWit2x protocol. Anyone who owns bitcoins at the time of the fork will then own both of these coins.

But this could also mean that most transactions will be equally valid on both blockchains. Whenever anyone wants to send coins on one chain, this exact same transaction could be "replayed" on the other chain, meaning both types of coins are actually spent on both chains, even if it was unintentional. This is known as a "replay attack" and can easily lead to a loss of funds.

These replay attacks can be prevented if BTC1 implements "replay protection." But as it currently stands, the BTC1 team has no intention of implementing such protection; at least, not in such a way that would properly solve the problem.

This lack of relay protection is considered disruptive and even reckless, not only by the opponents of the hard fork but also by several signatories of the NYA: some have already dropped out for this specific reason.

NO to brand confusion

Aside from replay protection, another big problem in the case of a coin-split could be brand confusion between the two types of coins. If users (and service providers) on both sides of the split consider their coin to be the "real" Bitcoin, it's not hard to imagine how this could lead to all sorts of complications. Users could, for example, buy one type of coin from an exchange even though they meant to buy another. Or they could send one type of coin to a merchant while they should have sent another. And so forth.

Such confusion could easily lead to a loss of funds, and perhaps even lawsuits and similar problems. (Even with Bitcoin Cash — which did pick a somewhat new name and added replay protection but not a new address format — there are many cases of confused users sending bitcoins to Bitcoin Cash addresses and the other way round.)

Opponents of SegWit2x maintain that it's the coin that results from this hard fork — the coin that follows a new protocol — that should pick a new name. But so far, NYA signatories have shown no willingness to do so.

NO to keeping a broken agreement

While the intent of the NYA was to keep the Bitcoin network together, SegWit2x opponents consider this agreement to have essentially been broken since.

Segregated Witness did activate on the Bitcoin network, probably in part thanks to SegWit2x, but also instigated by the BIP 148 UASF. However, some proponents of a block size limit increase hard fork (and opponents of SegWit) also launched Bitcoin Cash in response.

This realized a "split" between the Bitcoin and Bitcoin Cash blockchain and currency, not unlike the split Bitcoin Unlimited could have effectuated. Several NYA signatories — including Bitmain and Bitcoin.com — now support this fork, which SegWit2x opponents contend would nullify the original SegWit2x goal.

On top of that, several other signatories have since formally withdrawn their support, either because of the aforementioned lack of replay protection or for other reasons.

SegWit2x opponents therefore argue that the agreement, for all intents and purposes, has been broken and that there is no reason for the remaining signatories to keep to it.

NO to miners being the deciding factor.

And finally, SegWit2x opponents believe that its proponents misunderstand how Bitcoin consensus and incentives work.

Instead of setting the protocol rules, SegWit2x opponents maintain that miners need to follow the protocol rules, as enforced by users and their full-node clients. If miners mined blocks that are incompatible with the Bitcoin protocol as defined by users, these miners would not really be mining Bitcoin at all. Instead, the "blocks" they'd produce would simply be rejected by the network of users, and these miners would be mining a different coin at best or wasting their hash power at worst.

And again, this is not just a matter of principle. If miners were to decide which protocol is valid simply by dedicating hash power to it, it would imply that they can change any protocol rules. This would even let them change the inflation schedule to remove the 21 million coin limit, steal funds and more.

Indeed, it's no coincidence that the NO2X protest movement has much overlap with the BIP 148 UASF initiative: both maintain that users are in charge. Users decide which coin they want to buy, accept for payment and/or hold. As such, users decide which protocol is (more) valuable to dedicate hash power to the original Bitcoin protocol or the SegWit2x protocol. This is the protocol that miners will want to mine; not the other way round.

CHAPTER 10

BITCOIN: THREATS

Transaction time

One of the greatest threats to the mass adoption and long-term sustainability of Bitcoin is transaction time. According to Blockchain.com, in December 2017, it would take a *minimum* of sixty minutes and *up to* one hundred and twenty minutes to confirm a Bitcoin transaction.

Blockchain technology is not currently sufficiently geared for widespread or mass use. Transaction times are taking longer during peak periods because of block limits. The greater the interest in Bitcoin, the greater the number of bottlenecks that are being formed in the blockchain network. Altcoins such as Litecoin are already offering faster transaction times, and miners are looking to these coins as alternatives.

Hard forking creates the possibility of central authority control problems due to disagreements between miners.

Satoshi Nakamoto intended Bitcoin (and cryptocurrencies in general) to be decentralised with no interference, but if the miners collude and reach an agreement to hard fork, it becomes a form of central control. This would contradict the concept of decentralisation. Where the miners cannot reach agreement, the principle of decentralisation would be further reinforced. When hard forking is approved on a regular basis in an effort to make things faster or more effective, it could result in breaches to the software's intended design and function, which could, in turn, jeopardise the security and workings of Bitcoin and the blockchain.

There may be a partial solution for Bitcoin with the proposed Lightning Network that will be launched in the near future. This network would allow for multiple transactions to - and from outside - the blockchain by incorporating a second layer on top of the existing distributed ledger.

Transaction fees

Many believe that Bitcoin is a highly efficient method of exchange, but I beg to differ. In my opinion, it is already too expensive and too slow to operate as a transactional medium and it will become even more unaffordable as a trading currency in the future if alternative methods are not found to control transaction costs (such as the 'Lightning Coin' I referred to above), especially when it comes to day-to-day purchases. According to data provided by BitInfoCharts (at the time of writing this book), the average cost to approve a transaction was $8, increasing to up to $28 for urgent transactions.

It would not be outside of the norm to find users paying a $16 fee for sending $25 worth of Bitcoin, making the cost of using Bitcoin prohibitive for daily transactions. Aaron Lasher from Breadwallet (a 2014 Bitcoin wallet startup) experienced this on 4 August 2017 and was quite gobsmacked.

In 2009, Bitcoin was hailed as making micro-payments and money transfers cheaper than Western Union and other American banks. Ryan Charles, owner and founder of the San Francisco-based social media platform Yours Inc., was reported by CoinDesk to having moved his business away from using Bitcoin as a payment method when his fees increased nineteen-fold, from thirteen cents per average transaction to a staggering $2.40, becoming more expensive than using PayPal or Western Union.

Transaction costs are substantially higher than they were during Bitcoin's inception due to more people using or buying into the cryptocurrency. This is also directly correlated to increased demand and slow supply. Bottlenecks begin to form as Bitcoin owners try to push to the front of the queue by paying additional (or higher fees) to have their transactions validated faster by the miners.

The general consensus is that any transaction cost above $2 is not consumer-friendly, as confirmed by Shaun Chong, the lead developer at the mining community Bitcoin.com Pool. On the 29th of September 2017, the average price of a Bitcoin transaction was $2.46. This increase in transaction fees above the $2 mark was driven by an overloading of the network with high demand and short supply. As demand-and-supply and miners play a bigger role and further forks take place and scarcity builds, it is uncertain exactly how high transaction fees could become. There is, however, no question around the fact that is already too expensive as it is.

A partial solution is thought to be Bitcoin Cash, Bitcoin Gold with Segwit2, and the proposed 'Lightning Network'. Fees would remain high, but their increase would slow down due to the ongoing high demand and short supply. This is especially true when one considers that there are less than five million Bitcoins left to mine.

For large transactions, the high transaction fees would not be a major concern of businesses (or for criminals), but for the man on the street holding smaller numbers of Bitcoins, the fees could become prohibitive, especially when used as a payment tool instead of an investment vehicle.

For Bitcoin to go mainstream, it must be able to function with micro and macro scaling. Imagine buying a Starbucks coffee for $2.10, and then having to add the $2+ transaction fee on top of it?

Satoshi's vision of a cost-effective payment system is dissipating as transaction fees climb. It is indeed evolving into a store of value (through the *hodling* and hoarding of Bitcoins), similar to gold in years gone by, but with no intrinsic value.

Some of Bitcoin's main features have unfixable bugs, and its price volatility makes it unsustainable. Any currency that is used as a payment method should have the function of a store of value that is stable in relation to a basket of goods over time.

Can Bitcoin's volatility place it in the same category as money, or is it preferable to classify it as an 'asset'? With the believers hoarding the 'currency', consumerism – in terms of cryptocurrency – would slip out the back door and economic growth would be hampered because people would be hoarding their money rather than spending it. The currency-turned-asset could become a major liability to any economy and would even go against the founding members' white paper principles. Bitcoin must be used as a digital currency and not as a high-risk investment. The system is fundamentally flawed at present in that it continues to suck people into it in order to fund its value as an asset rather than a currency.

Cryptocurrency miners are, in my opinion, the real winners for now. The current wave of cryptomania could come to an abrupt end at any given time, but if the miners use their window of opportunity wisely, they can make sufficient money to cover their large upfront capital outlays and still see a reasonable return on their investment in order to pay their overhead costs and make a profit. My guess is that this would be all about timing.

A powerful crypto mining rig with optimum power capabilities could set a miner back in the region of 300 000 – 1 000 000 ZAR. The high costs of power consumption associated with these mining servers will take a significant bite out of the miner's net profit. Miners who are able to secure these costs - both through fees and also through selling the Bitcoins they receive as rewards – could be set up for powerful passive income streams, with the only risk being Bitcoin failing, or the price falling below the breakeven point

Individuals who cannot afford these types of Bitcoin mining rigs may consider the many other more accessible cryptocurrencies where a lower capital outlay is required. It is important to remember that mining involves high power consumption due to the hardware's cooling off requirements and that these costs need to be taken into account in terms of the miner's earning capacity.

Bitcoin miners are making money hand over fist when the price of Bitcoin is above the breakeven level above $ 8 000. Seven percent of the total value stored in Bitcoin comes from rewards (remunerations) paid to miners. Each time a miner validates a transaction, new coins are created to pay the miner (similar to the banks printing paper money with nothing of value to back that piece of paper). At the time of writing this book, miners were receiving a reward of 12.5 Bitcoins per block that they opened up. The reward for mining a Bitcoin block halves every 210 000 blocks. This means that the reward after the next halving will be 6.25 coins per block. For additional information, and for some great statistics on the working of halving, as well as a countdown to the next halving which is expected to take place around the 31st of May 2018, please visit www.bitcoinblockhalf.com

Miners also receive transaction fees when transactions are made on their block. According to Blockchain.com data, $11 million was paid to miners in transactions fees on a single day during 2017.

Many Bitcoin owners are turning to altcoins because of their lower fees, but those who are happy with Bitcoin as a store of value are sticking to Bitcoin and purchasing more of them. When one does not transact, or transacts only when one sells ones Bitcoins, transaction fees are irrelevant.

According to the live countdown on the bitcoinblockhalf.com website at 20:15 pm on 11 March 2018, the figures were as follows:

- 16 913 138 – The total Bitcoins issued since 2009
- 80.54% – The percentage of Bitcoins mined to date
- 4 086 863 – The total Bitcoins left to mine over the next 112 years
- $9.606 – The current Bitcoin price
- 3.96% – The current annual Bitcoin inflation rate (It will be 1.80% at the next halving)
- 513 051 – The total blocks mined to date
- 116 949 – The total number of blocks to be mined before the mining reward is halved again
- 1 461 863 – The total number of Bitcoins to be mined until the next blockhalf

- 10 minutes – The approximate time to mine one block

These incredible figures are changing continuously with the mining process.

Regulations

It was during January 2018 that we saw some glimpses of significant regulatory impacts on Bitcoin. In fact, I would venture to state that as 2017 was the year of Bitcoin coming alive as a household name, 2018 would be known as the year of regulatory impact on Bitcoin.

The US Securities and Exchange Commission is investigating ICOs under their securities platform and has already charged one individual and a couple of companies with fraud. The SEC gave notice in March 2018 that online trading platforms that serve as digital assets (securities) would need to register with the agency in order to allow for regulatory oversight. If these platforms feel that they do not qualify as national exchanges, they would have to apply for an exemption. The SEC believes that this would prevent the misrepresentation of the word 'exchange' which is used by many ICO tokens and crypto exchanges without meeting regulatory requirements.

Governments and institutions worldwide are concerned with cryptocurrency. Consider what has happened in China and South Korea with ICOs and exchanges being referred to as concocted pyramid schemes, with criminal activities disguised as scientific and technological innovation.

Swiss regulator FINMA recently joined China and South Korea and called for investigations into fraudulent activities associated with ICOs, in particular, fake cryptocurrencies like E-Coin.

Influential people (who hold massive wealth and have no reason to pursue get-rich-quick schemes) like JPMorgan's CEO Jamie Dimon, Bridgewater Associates Ray Dalio, Morgan Stanley's CEO James Garner, Blackrock's CEO Larry Fink, UBS' Chairman Axel Weber, UBS Wealth Management's Paul Donovan, along with billionaires Howard Marks and Warren Buffet, and even South Africa's own legendary economist, Mike Schussler, have referred to Bitcoin using terms like *fraudulent*, *bubbles*, *schemes*, *bull*, *disaster*, *thin air*, *nothing*, *hype*, *complex* and *manipulation*, to name but a few.

Nations like Bolivia, Ecuador, South Korean, Sweden, Thailand, Ukraine, India, and Namibia are all considering banning crypto and exchanges in the future.

On the same day that the SEC made their announcement, Japan's financial services agency ordered two exchanges (FSHO and Bit Station) to halt trading. It penalised four others (GMO Internet Inc., GMO Coin, Tech Bureau Corp, Zaif, Bicrement and Mr. Exchange), with further possible sanctions to follow. This was an interesting development, with Japan being only one of a handful of governments that currently has a licensing system for crypto exchanges.

It is, however, not surprising when one considers the over $500 million hack of Tokyo-based Coincheck Inc. in January 2018. This incident, together with other similar events, has resulted in the Japanese Government (through its financial Regulator), approving increased stringent controls over exchanges, with considerably more oversight from the Regulator.

The European Central Bank's (ECB) President Mario Draghi made a powerful statement in 2017, saying that crypto cannot be regulated by the ECB under its current laws. Draghi stated that it would be premature to consider crypto as legal tender in the future. He went on to say that the ECB may review both Bitcoin and the blockchain as the industry matures but, until then, the European Union (EU) states that Estonia must stay in line. As a result of this, Estonia's plans to launch a state-backed cryptocurrency fell flat on its back, since no new or country-own currencies can be approved without the EU's permission.

Draghi referred to the Tulip Mania that took place in the Netherlands in the 1600s as an example of what could go wrong. He stated that the ECB did not see cryptocurrency as a threat to the EU's financial sector because the EU does not view it as a currency. When one considers what happened in China, there is a possibility that Draghi could be wrong.

With so many powerful executives and people with clout voicing their opinions on Bitcoin (with little being voiced on the merits and demerits of the blockchain), the noise is becoming increasingly louder. This is mostly due to the fact that there are limited regulations in place currently.

The believers are fighting tooth and nail not to be included under a securities platform regulated by the SEC, but with a mind-boggling array of ICO listings, over eighty-five crypto hedge funds and more than one thousand five hundred cryptocurrencies (and counting), the question remains whether intervention is required at all, whether it is even possible to have a decentralised, self-regulated system or whether it requires, at minimum, some level of macro-regulation.

At a Senate hearing in February 2018, US regulators agreed on a 'do no harm' approach to cryptocurrencies. This was a simple decision, but, because it was seen as positive news, it had a far-reaching impact in helping to hype the price upwards after the major correction that took place in January 2018.

If Bitcoin and Ethereum are here to stay, the SEC will have to declare ICOs as securities (because they have no effective technology utility), and this would result in a significant drop in new ICOs coming into the market to continue funding and driving the crypto industry. Many believe that this would assist the new industry to mature with real sustainability.

The most significant regulatory threat, in my opinion, would come about when the G8 and G20 countries add cryptocurrencies and blockchain technology to their agendas. Christine Lagarde, head of the IMF (International Monetary Fund), recently stated that authorities around the world should harness the potential of cryptocurrencies to help bring them under control.

She warned that not doing so would allow the unfettered development of a 'potential major new vehicle for money laundering and the financing of terrorism' to thrive. She also stated that it would also help to mitigate 'financial vulnerability' in the world. Lagarde clearly believes in the opportunities that the blockchain brings with it as a low-cost payment method for those without bank accounts, as well as how it can revolutionise financial services.

The trading of Bitcoins cannot be stopped, but the process can be impeded by governments and institutions that can make it illegal to buy or sell Bitcoins using local currencies. They could also simply stop the exchanges from using local currencies to convert the Bitcoins, as was seen recently with China banning ICOs, with South Korean hot on its heels. This may result in miners not being able to sell coins they make from mining to maintain their infrastructure and services until other countries take up the mining.

On the opposite end of the spectrum, the level of *decentralisation* or *deregulation* of Bitcoin is largely dependent on the miners agreeing to any software, mining (or other) changes and if they can reach agreement in terms of whether to create hard forks or not.

I believe that as long as the miners (who are forming more and more groups due to the complexity and costs associated with the mining process) are involved, Bitcoin cannot be perceived as completely fulfilling the principles of a decentralised system. Although it has not been factually proven, it appears that between eight and ten groups control eighty percent of the coins being mined. Does this give these groups of miners' undue power to influence the system? This does, in fact, seem to be the case when we look at the process of hard forking.

Tax Implications are a huge threat to governments and therefore to Bitcoin as well. Limited tax is being paid at present, and I can only assume that it is because people are holding on to their Bitcoins. It could also be that treasuries and tax bodies have not yet figured out how to tax cryptocurrencies or crypto assets, or whatever it will be defined as in each country over time. Tax activities cannot be triggered if the coins are not being sold or spent. The problem could also be the design of the blockchain which makes the details associated with transactions anonymous.

Bitcoin investors, as with any other investor, *should* be taxed, especially with Bitcoin being referred to as an asset class (and not a currency) due to its hybrid system that combines the advantages of money with debt and equity. The notion is that where Bitcoin is used as a digital currency for transactional purposes, it should be taxed in the same way as a transaction that is paid for using a traditional currency. In this instance, we would be looking at sales tax (or VAT). The problem is where Bitcoin is not (currently) seen by most governments as legal tender, versus where governments *do* consider it as legal tender – such as in Japan.

The issue with taxation will be resolved through regulations in the future, but cryptocurrency owners would be advised to allow for the tax liability resulting from any asset growth between when they are purchased and when the coins are eventually sold, as well as any transactions made with Bitcoin.

There is a myriad of complex definitions of what Bitcoin represents, and it would be up to each country's treasury to determine under which tax group Bitcoin would fall. Once a country eventually defines the type of tax to be paid, it will be interesting to see how the crypto millionaires and billionaires are going to pay their taxes if Bitcoin is not seen as legal tender in their country. Would the government of their country accept Bitcoin as a means of payment for income tax, VAT, Capital Gains Tax, and how would the taxpayer convert these large sums of money into physical cash or fiat currency in time to pay the taxman?

News hot off the press in March 2018 was that Bitcoin owners trading in the USA would become liable for hefty capital gains tax for trading profits made during 2017. In 2014, the USA Internal Revenue Service (IRS) announced that Bitcoin and other cryptocurrencies would be treated as property, rather than currency, and would be taxed accordingly.

With the price of Bitcoin more than halving since these profits were made, crypto owners may not have enough capital to pay their taxes. Because the IRS certainly does not accept Bitcoin as a form of payment, this could force Bitcoin owners to sell at nominal prices as a means of ensuring some liquidity in order to make these tax payments.

There are some Bitcoin owners who are using the coin's low price to prevent excessive capital gains for the 2018 tax year. In the USA, these taxes – seen as short-term capital gains - can be as high as 39%, depending on the individual's tax bracket. The dilemma comes about when the long-term capital gain – when it is held for longer than one year – is taxed at only 20% (on average). For the young millennials who have made gains beyond their wildest expectations, but with very little concern about tax affairs, or who do not understand the investment market and its complex tax impacts, this becomes problematic and will require some tough decisions to be made.

It goes without saying that anyone purchasing Bitcoins should proactively familiarise themselves with the tax implications of buying, selling, trading and spending Bitcoin, and to make tax payments without building up an escalated tax liability with their local tax office, regardless of whether the profits are made locally or globally.

The percentage of profit or what type of tax is to be paid is a question that will remain mostly unanswered for the next couple of years, but I believe that governments will start waking up from 2018 and start becoming clearer on the tax impacts of cryptocurrency.

Cryptocurrency owners should not assume that by simply allocating some of the Bitcoins in their electronic wallets to the taxman that they will be in a position to physically pay such taxes when the time comes. Liquidity could be problematic, or the price could fall significantly year on year, leaving the owner with a tax deficit to pay, or they might be forced to sell at a low price and take a loss on the future opportunity cost in order to pay their taxed, thereby creating an unfortunate double negative.

In terms of advice from financial professionals and tax professionals, it is doubtful whether there are many of these professionals who would be willing to put their fiduciary duties and fidelity insurance on the line to give an opinion or to rule on Bitcoin tax implications at this early stage of transformation of the ecosystem. As a Certified Tax Practitioner with SAIT, I would most certainly not do so, and as a Certified Financial Planner with FPI, I would not provide advice on crypto under my professional licence and code of conduct and ethics either. This does not mean that I have not been inundated with requests over the past two years; in fact, it is the main reasons that I decided to write this educational non-advice book in the first place.

Ecosystem

An ecosystem is a process that evolves over time. There is simply not enough of an ecosystem at present to allow analysts to study the fundamentals and principles of Bitcoin. The more the ecosystem evolves, the stronger Bitcoin can become, but attempting to fast-track an ecosystem to give it maturity and credibility you risk placing it under considerable threat.

In this ecosystem, competitors, newer technology, and new digital currencies with superior technology are all important. Ethereum is likely to be Bitcoin's greatest threat as a competitor because, not only is it a cryptocurrency, it is also a blockchain platform on which various other applications can be built, such as smart contracts. Smart contracts are self-executing digital contracts that control the transfer of assets or cryptocurrencies to and between various parties when certain 'If-Then' conditions are met, obviating the need for traditional paper-based supply chain systems that require human approval as the forms move through the system.

Bitcoin should not become too comfortable with its majority position. Remember Yahoo before Google, and Myspace before Facebook? Not many people took an outside bet on the Internet of the 1990s, and they lost out. Who will be betting on cryptocurrency (in an evolved format) and blockchain becoming bigger than the internet? My suggestion would be to place your bets before it is too late.

Algorithms

The codes that make up cryptocurrency's codes are complex – probably the most advanced algorithms created in the world to date - and far too slow to authenticate transactions, especially when one considers the possible use of cryptocurrencies for business transactions in the future. Microsoft may have some solutions, but it is too early to tell.

Scams

Scams are a major threat to Bitcoin. There are far too many ICOs popping up, with an estimated seventy percent (or more) of them that could be perceived as scams or Ponzi schemes of some form or other.

Without regulators being involved, you will always be on your own. If you get scammed during a Bitcoin transaction, or by an exchange or an ICO, or through the loss of your electronic wallet, you have no recourse. This is simply a side effect of transaction outside of a regulated environment.

Fraud is a virtual game, and the largest virtual bank robbery will probably take place sooner than we think. It is only once security is bedded down as loopholes are discovered, and education is driven by the ecosystem, that instances of fraud can be mitigated. It is said that a blockchain is at its most vulnerable to be hacked when it first comes online, but the length of time of this vulnerability is unclear. With the blockchain having been in place since 2009, it may already have survived its most vulnerable period.

The increase in price and the growth in volumes of virtual currencies allows unscrupulous operators to lure potential investors into Ponzi schemes with their promises of wealth through their get-rich-quick branding schemes. This is especially true in instances where Bitcoin values saw rapid growth in short bursts. Some of these operators who draw people in without fear are GainBitcoin, Shavers, and Gaw Miners.

Although I do not believe that Bitcoin (in itself) is a scam, the manner in which Bitcoin is sold could be perceived as a scam because it has no intrinsic value; it is simply an allocated number that is being sold. Its value does not lie in the number itself, but rather in the perceived value between two parties (peer-to-peer).

The lack of a middleman - which allow for savings on cost and fees – may be perceived as valuable. The fact that Bitcoin is unique with a finite number of coins available may possibly hold some value, but if every coin is simply a number, one has to consider that there can never be a shortage of numbers, especially if somebody comes up with a similar concept and starts creating more numbers.

The amount of numbers generated can only be limited by the mathematicians' ability to create the algorithms. The number of algorithms that can be generated is infinite. I believe that to claim a finite supply of coins is only possible if Bitcoin is the only cryptocurrency in the world at any given time.

As we reach the end of this SWOT analysis, it should be clear that there is indeed a strong case for the blockchain, and a *bit* of a case for some cryptocurrencies. The case *for* cryptocurrencies is only strong (in my opinion) if they are to be used in their intended form as a transactional or payment tool. If Bitcoin was *only* used as a transactional tool or a digital coin, I believe that there would be an exceptional case for Bitcoin and some of its competitor coins.

For people out there wanting to make the proverbial quick buck, there is ample opportunity in cryptocurrency, just as long as they are prepared for a ride that is peppered with high risk and inherent volatility, and the possibility of a complete loss of capital.

CHAPTER 11

INVESTING IN CYPTOCURRENCY
THE SMART ANALYSIS

It is important to remember that there are always opportunities when manias, volatility and potential bubbles are taking centre stage.

For those who read through the SWOT analysis in detail and still feel that they want to bite into the coin, being SMART should always come before being greedy. For these brave people, this chapter will make for interesting reading from a non-advice point of view.

Before I continue, I would like to once again emphasise that, as a financial advisor, I would not recommend that any of my clients buy into Bitcoin or any form of cryptocurrency. Should they go ahead and dive in anyway (as has already happened with some of my clients, where significant losses of between R250 000 and R1 200 000 were made), it would be at their discretion. I would simply wish them the best of luck since, in my opinion, it is akin to visiting a casino and placing your bets against the house.

Once they have learned the hard lessons, I am certain that we can rebuild their wealth through proven long-term methods, using the power of (Einstein's) eighth wonder of the world: Compound interest.

Specific

Be specific with your objectives - especially with the *Whys* and the *Hows* - and stay away from altcoins and ICOs if you have not done sufficient due diligence and understand exactly what the purpose and risk of each coin is.

Diversification is always an option, and a combination of Bitcoin and Ethereum for direct access (i.e. not via an ICO – or similar) would increase the odds in your favour. For those who have a knack for being able to identify and sniff out legitimate altcoins and ICOs, the moon could be in range, as we saw with the top ten returns in 2017 of up to 33 000%. If these returns can be converted into real fiat money at any given time, without restriction, it would move beyond simply being 'fictitious' money.

Indirect access into companies making use of Distributed Ledger Technology (DLT) – in other words, the Blockchain -

or other decentralised innovations such as Smart Contracts would reduce exposure. Using a hedge fund route as an alternative option, leaving it to the experts to double up on your safety, but with lower returns (although still spectacular when compared to anything else we know) would be more prudent.

Buying in on a Rand average costing basis would be good practice as a means of buffering the massive volatility associated with cryptocurrency. It would be deemed highly negligent to have exposure at more than two to five percent of your total investment portfolio. Using unencumbered cash and being willing to say goodbye to it at any given time would help to ease the pain you can expect. When I say "it", I mean up to one hundred percent of its value, including any gains.

Taking profits (if you are able to cash in on time) on an ongoing basis and when a particular cryptocurrency is on the up would be beneficial if you wish to reduce the risk rating and ensure that liquidity passes the normal restrictions.

Very few exchanges would allow a 100% mandate order on the sale of bulk crypto as it would drain the cash flow and liquidity of such exchanges, and, as such, most exchanges have restrictions on bulk sales.

Measure

If you are playing the cryptocurrency market on your own (and purely on a speculative basis and not as a payment tool), then daily - and even hourly - measurements should form part of your habits due to cryptocurrency's flash volatility concerns. Bitcoin and Ethereum trend charts will ensure that you are vigilant (and stressed) on the down, and excited on the up.

Allocation

For experienced investors, it should be clear that a well-balanced portfolio may allow for a relatively small allocation of Bitcoin and Ethereum to boost the potential on your short-term strategy. The stock market is always a gamble, and this part of your portfolio will be a gamble *on steroid*s.

To allow exposure above 5%, and certainly not as high as 80%, as I witnessed a financial advisor writing about openly in a recent publication, would simply be negligent. Imagine the message that he is sending out, both to his client base and to the public, not to mention the fiduciary liability that he is placing himself under.

I believe such advisors will be stress-tested in the future by the ombuds office under their professional status held in the public domain, and quite possibly while Bitcoin is an unregulated product.

There is always room for precedent cases, and the FAIS act still holds financial advisors to advise within the limits of their professional status.

The direct storing of money into any 'investment' vehicle should correlate directly with the level of an investment's volatility, and balance sheet protection should always take preference, with some consideration to risk profiling. Avoiding being greedy (holding on with the hope of future gains) by taking profits from the top could reduce exposure.

The saying "If you don't understand it, don't invest in it", rings true, and is one of the reasons why Warren Buffet – world-renowned investor - is not interested in investing in Bitcoin. His reasoning is that he does not understand nor does he appreciate the opportunity or its underlying technology. If the greatest global bankers and investment gurus like Warren Buffet do not understand it, what chance does the retail investor have? Even worse, what about the uneducated investor who is simply following a herd mentality?

Considering there are over 1500 coins and way too many ICOs, compounded by concerns over certain exchanges, conducting any due diligence studies could prove to be difficult.

Major losses already experienced by Bitfinex, Mt. Cox, and Coincheck, should signal warning bells in terms of the dangers that could potentially await you.

Realise profits

Objectively speaking, it may be prudent to set realistic expectations and keep the greed monster at arm's length from one's emotions when it comes to investing in cryptocurrency.

Once you have this under control, you would need to follow a carefully-considered decision-making process on taking profits, including how and when to take them. You may even want to define your own lower and upper threshold levels.

By realising profits and recovering your originally-invested capital, you would likely reduce your downside risk.

Time

As all my clients and my followers are aware, I do not (under normal investment principles) believe in timing anything when it comes to my clients investments, apart from when it comes to my personal (proven) share portfolio where I am willing to take my own risks with once-off opportunities in stocks on the down (Dimension Data, Old Mutual, Steinhoff, EOH, Pinnacle, Capitec, Lonmin, African Bank, to name but a few). I prefer to spend time *in* the market rather than timing the markets. In terms of cryptocurrency, and from an objective standpoint, skimming profits from the top appears to be *all* about timing. Even the length of time that you remain involved in crypto would be about timing.

The volatility associated with cryptocurrency is completely different due to its short-term and immediate volatility (which is associated with *any* good or bad news through social media hype). This most certainly allows for timing opportunities, which is how the big Bitcoin boys turn the millions into billions, only to find out a couple of weeks later that they are millionaires again, and not billionaires. I must add, however, that many have done this with an admirable level of patience since Bitcoin's inception in 2009, and some because they simply forgot that they had Bitcoin stashed away, and woke up to them when the price went crazy.

During 2017, and while writing this book, I decided to experiment with 'predicting' negative and positive corrections on the Bitcoin price. Let's call it trendspotting, for lack of a better word. I posted four predictions on LinkedIn on possible percentage corrections, and within an average of four days, I got close to all four over time, with some being very close. Similar to share trading, and had I been trading in Bitcoin, it could have resulted in significant personal financial gains.

When I made my fifth prediction, I decided to be overconfident, 'predicting' both the percentage in upswing *and* in the value of the price range. This time I was only correct on the percentage upswing because the market experienced a further upward flash in terms of value, which resulted in the price rising above my prediction on percentage upward correction.

Was my accuracy based on pure luck, or was it based on a deeper understanding of Bitcoin, or even my years of stock trading experience? I can only put it down to luck because I do not believe that Bitcoin's performance can be predicted at all. In fact, nobody has been able to make consistently good price predictions to date.

CHAPTER 12

CONCLUSION
A SUMMARY OF THE SWOT AND SMART ANALYSIS

Crypto is here to stay!

Investors (whether long-term or first-time) should try to stay away from crypto until the ecosystem has matured and has been stress-tested. This market should only be entered once you completely understand the underlying technology and its associated risk.

Investors must appreciate the importance of upcoming regulatory changes and the associated tax implications. There will still be an opportunity once *somebody* has been able to define what the phenomenon actually is (or will be) in the future; whether it is a currency, a store of value, an asset class, or an investment, rather than what Bitcoin is in its current form.

Crypto is here to stay, and Crypto 2.0 and 3.0 will evolve over time and be utilised as a true payment and transaction method. This could push Crypto 1.0 out of the mainstream. Bitcoin could probably be the biggest loser if this is the case, unless, of course, it has morphed into Bitcoin Crypto 2.0 itself.

Cryptomania and the blockchain will do for virtual money and transactions what the Railway Mania (an economic bubble that involved a frenzy in railroad development and in speculation in railroad shares) did for the rail and transport industry in the 1850s, and what email did to the fax and the post office in the 1990s. Some good may emerge from certain bubbles or mania. The Railway Mania bubble was such a bubble because it created some indirect positive outcomes for the future of humankind, despite the fact that many people lost their life savings, or became bankrupt in the process.

Could cryptocurrency replace fiat currency? I am of the opinion that cryptocurrency can *complement* fiat currency and in some instances *replace* certain functionalities of fiat money, but that it could not during the course of our lifetimes replace it completely, is a fact. This is something that could only happen beyond our lifetime in the far distant future, and only if it becomes more effective, efficient and trustworthy than fiat money, and returning to its core intentions as a payment vehicle.

Because crypto is here to stay, it would be important for portfolio managers to appreciate and understand crypto at its worst - which is as it currently stands - so that when Crypto 2.0, 3.0 (and so forth) evolve within a more regulated environment in the future, then they can add value to their fund mandates.

When it comes to Bitcoin, will it remain for the time being, until there is an alternative? Bitcoin appears to be highly resilient, and if it was going to disappear (by becoming a bubble), it would have disappeared by now, especially when one considers the major disruptions it has faced, with China and then the impact made by comments from various high profile international executives. It has been a revelation to see it fight against all odds.

Perhaps it is indeed a revolution in progress, and, similarly, perhaps there is still time to make money in it, or to buy a couple of things with it.

Cryptocurrency is really a solution looking for a problem to solve, and it should focus on the problem it found; being a decentralised alternative to centralised fiat money and governments controls.

There is no doubt that we should thank the creators of Bitcoin and the blockchain for developing the blockchain's underlying technology. This will be a blockbuster during the Fourth Industrial Revolution, and possibly have a far greater impact than the *Internet of things*, even overshadowing other major disruptors such as social media, AI (Artificial Intelligence), robotics, nanotechnology, and so forth with its massive potential. We can only hope that if Bitcoin - in its current inherently flawed form - does not survive, that the blockchain finds mass adoption before then in order to continue beyond Bitcoin.

Blockchain (as a world without middlemen) holds huge potential, and this alone should allow for a standalone platform. If we add the potential for huge cost savings to various industries, there should be no reason why the blockchain could not have a bright future as a global, borderless game changer. In my opinion, there is no turning back on the blockchain, and it will find mass adoption in upcoming years, and its uses will move far beyond that of crypto and smart contracts only.

This quote from Ginni Rometty, the current CEO of IBM, sums it up perfectly:

"What the Internet did for communications, I think blockchain will do for trusted transactions."

The general feeling is that the blockchain is now where the Internet was twenty years ago, with only 0.5% of the world's population using it. In 2017, 51% of the world's population was using the Internet.

Onerous

The technology associated with Bitcoin and the blockchain is onerous to understand, but the more you know, the more you can take advantage of its opportunities.

If you do not understand it, as Warren Buffett says, don't invest in it.

Natural evolution

Bitcoin and crypto must evolve naturally through a sound ecosystem. Similarly, it appears that the natural evolution of currency has arrived in the unstoppable form of cryptocurrencies and blockchain.

James Altucher, an American hedge fund manager and author, was quoted on his website in August 2017 as saying,

"BC will stand for "Before Crypto", and AC will stand for "After Crypto". We are in AC right now, and the world is about to change."

Although I like his philosophy, I would not agree with the 'AC' period for now. I am certain that the 'BC' period will evolve into the 'AC' period in the next twenty years.

Classic bubble

A great deal of money is going into something that only a few understand. For the uneducated and the uninformed, their primary concern is not an appreciation of its complex structures, but rather that greater volumes of money are flowing into the system.

More and more people are looking to move away from 'untrusted' banks and middlemen. The human touch is, however, still relevant throughout the ecosystem. People do not want to re-live the Subprime losses or the Dotcom crash, yet there are ongoing losses when one takes a look at Bitcoin's volatility over the past couple of months, especially if you take the crash from a record high of close to $20 0000, down to below $6000 in January 2018, into consideration.

Crypto appears to be in a trading bubble (and in a state of mania) because of its unreasonable and unrealistically high prices. This is impossible to sustain in terms of basic economic and investment principles. Once the bubble bursts there will be a plethora of millionaires, billionaires and wealthy people created from that brave first wave of entrepreneurs, skilled investors and hedge fund managers (and similar). Sadly, however, there will be millions of unsophisticated 'investors' – those who followed the herd and then hoarded their coins - who will lose their life savings and become penniless in the same way that people did more than four hundred years ago during the period of Tulip Mania, and the many bubbles since.

During periods of volatility, when the herd panics and runs, selling on the down, the heartless 'traders' - who know how to read graphs and charts, while ignoring the noise and emotions, climb in and take advantage of these profit-making opportunities. They buy in at the low and sell at the high, something that, in Bitcoin's case, is a great deal easier to control than in normal markets (which move significantly slower, and with underlying value).

Bitcoin, with no intrinsic value, moves a great deal faster, moving upwards or downwards in the range of $2000 in a matter of hours.

The bottom line is that bubbles bring enormous opportunities. Depending on where you are operating from, these bubbles can be floated to incredibly high levels, and, with expert timing, they can be used to create unlimited wealth for some and, conversely, inconceivable losses for others.

Losers

One does not *invest* in Bitcoin; one *gambles* with it. As with any high-risk investment, you should, therefore, only invest as much as you are willing to lose. Any savvy financial advisor would tell you to think three times before letting go of your hard-earned capital and, if you do decide to take the risk, to ask yourself if you are willing to lose one hundred percent of your capital if something goes wrong. Old school financial advisors would likely suggest that you seek out regulated companies who are currently invested in blockchain technologies and who are trying to find alternative uses for the blockchain outside of cryptocurrencies (and subsequent coins).

The real winners in cryptocurrency are usually the miners, especially if they sell the 12.5 Bitcoins (the current reward payment for every block mined) that they receive as their reward per block as they mine it, and especially when the price is on the up. The losers are the 'investors' who are last in and who sell, in fear, on the down.

Advisors should be cautious when giving advice on such gambles under their fiduciary duties, both directly and indirectly.

We will come back to this point at the end of this book with regulatory input from Anton Swanepoel, Chair of The Financial Planning Committee of the FIA.

Ulterior motives

Bitcoin's ulterior and conflicting motives have moved far beyond the original principles of the founders. There are significant philosophical differences between those stakeholders who want Bitcoin to be a valuable digital asset class, and those who want to maintain the founder's white paper objective to use Bitcoin as a borderless and unregulated payment and transactional network.

These differences have created a great deal of infighting amongst miners, something that is completely out of line with the original founder's principles and intentions to come up with a Fourth Industrial Revolution Fintech tool, and a certain winner in terms of Blockchain technology.

Sweat it out

Guts, glory, a strong temperament and plenty of sweat are the ingredients required to take on a mania and a bubble.

Once you invest in crypto, you had better be prepared to sweat it out during the tough periods.

Integrity with ethics

It is unethical to support and promote an unregulated and unproven scheme if you know that money is at risk with the uneducated investor who is following all the hype, not to mention the herd.

The herd arrives late – driven by greed - and stays in, and then wakes up too late when the market is on the down and, driven by fear, proceeds to lose most or all of their investment when the bubble bursts or when the market experiences a major correction. The high profile and analytical financial gurus (and let's not forget the opportunists) love the herd mentality because it is precisely that which helps drive price levels up in order to allow for substantial profit-taking.

There is no doubt there is money to be made, especially if you are shrewd enough to cash in from the top of the charts on a regular basis. Cashing in by skimming from the top on a regular basis means that you are ensuring that your profits are held in real money instead of virtual money.

There is no doubt that if cryptocurrency was a 'Ponzi scheme' or a pyramid scheme (which I do not believe it is), or if it fails because the core principles were deviated from (because a payment method became an asset class), and the software is failing it through price, fees and mining costs and scarcity, then somebody will always be losing money.

Are you willing to sacrifice your ethical principles under these circumstances?

Open mind on losses

Manias and bubbles can be profitable and as long as you keep an open mind in terms of accepting major losses as much as you accept making huge profits.

Ask yourself whether you are willing to throw it all away at any given time before you click on the *buy* button

Never say never

Can any one of us say that we will never do anything?

Although I have stated unequivocally and on numerous occasions throughout this book, as well as on social media, that I would never buy Bitcoins for myself (and would only ever consider it for reasons beyond personal gain or loss), I will at this point disclose that on the 9th of September 2017 I purchased Bitcoins for the first time. The only reason that I took this step was to empower myself with some direct knowledge in order to ensure a certain level of integrity (and personal experience) before writing the final chapters of this book.

I have since sold my Bitcoin holding, but I had a feeling that the Bitcoin Evangelists would come at me and shoot me down for not personally owning Bitcoins - or crypto in any form, and the reason why I had to experience the ecosystem myself in practice.

Within a few days of buying my first shares of Bitcoin, I received my first attack from a believer in an article (published on LinkedIn) defending Bitcoin after its negative worldwide press. The author of the article compared me to Jamie Dimon, which I will admit is an honour, considering his achievements. The author went on to say that I should not be trying to be clever about Bitcoin as if I have never traded in it. Fortunately, I could prove him wrong in this case.

I believe that it is my duty to examine and explain both sides of the coin rather than simply focussing on one side, waxing lyrical about its positives without considering the negatives, as so many other so-called experts are currently doing, and I can only hope that I have been able to do so in a complex and technical ecosystem.

CHAPTER 13

ARE YOU READY FOR CRYPTO-CONVERSATIONS?

This chapter is dedicated to those who work in the financial services profession, but will remain interesting reading for those who are clients of financial service professionals.

There is no doubt in my mind that if Bitcoin was recognised as an asset class – which is impossible as long as it remains unregulated – it would have won the award for best-performing asset class of 2017. Were it a recognised currency, it would have most certainly run away with the best performing currency of the year award.

However, if we were to ask a statistically-significant sample of the entire world's population (including people living in countries where there is no internet) whether they have ever heard of cryptocurrency, I suspect that responses in the affirmative would be on the low, even if we threw the words 'blockchain' and 'Bitcoin' in.

Taken a step further, if we were to ask those who *had* heard of it whether they had any understanding of it as a concept, I suspect that a positive response would border on something close to negligible.

Were we to change our hypothetical sample to include only our immediate clients and prospects, I would imagine that most of these people would agree that they have *heard* of the term cryptocurrency, but in as far as actually understanding the concept and how it works, a positive response will likely be on the lower side of the sample.

My sense is that many advisors would prefer to ignore this market disruptor and phenomenon because of its complexity. Some may genuinely see it as a threat to their clients' portfolios. Many might view cryptocurrency as a threat to their own business models which operate seamlessly with tried and tested regulated investment practices in place. After all, if it ain't broke, don't fix it, right?

In my opinion, it would be a mistake to ignore the impact of cryptocurrencies, and advisors that do, do so at their own peril. The blockchain and Bitcoin are out there, and some of our clients are reading up on and dabbling in this market. It is for this reason that it is our fiduciary duty as financial advisors and professionals, and especially as CFPs, to be fully up to date on the latest trends and developments in cryptocurrency and blockchain technologies if we are to be in a position to adequately answer our clients' questions, and address their concerns.

In fact, I would go as far as saying that we would be opening ourselves up to potential claims of negligence and associated liability if we *fail* to keep abreast of such trends. Whether you're a realist (sceptical about crypto) or a crypto-evangelist, you need to be aware of cryptocurrency, and, most importantly, you need to understand it.

It is imperative for us as financial professionals to educate ourselves on crypto technology in order to appreciate the impact that it could have on our clients' portfolios as 'investments' (but not before being regulated), both now and in the future. Similarly, we need to appreciate its impact on our advice practices and compliance duties. We cannot simply assume that under the FAIS Act, together with our own codes of conduct and ethics that our clients should not get involved with crypto simply because we view it as a potential bubble, Ponzi Scheme, or the latest quick money making scheme. An attitude of this nature could damage both our reputation and credibility. Imagine your client asking for your informed opinion when you don't have one?

It would be fair to note that if you do not stay up to date on cryptocurrencies and their associated blockchain technology – and even become an expert or thought leader on the subject – you may find yourself unable to protect your practice against those competitors who are on top of crypto happenings. Knowledge in this arena can only enhance your value proposition to your clients, but it would be paramount that you maintain a fine line between education and giving advice.

Keeping abreast of international and local regulatory changes on cryptocurrencies (from a legal and tax perspective) forms a critical part of ongoing professional education and knowledge. This phenomenon could become a huge disruptor within the financial service and banking industries, making robo-advice (as an earlier disruptor in the financial services industry) pale in significance when compared to this monster that is rearing its head.

The cross-border electronic payment component of Bitcoin that applies to individuals (and those of us who deal with SMEs within our businesses) also needs to be considered.

Irrespective of whether Bitcoin is used in a regulated environment or not, there are going to be tax implications.

In truth, we cannot assume that this new phenomenon will turn out to be the biggest financial disaster of the past four hundred years – or, for that matter, the best thing to happen in the Fourth Industrial Revolution. With the final Bitcoin only being mined in 2140, we have more than one hundred years (perhaps not all of us, depending on our age) to watch the story to play out.

I strongly encourage all members of the financial services sector - and advisors in particular - to be vigilant in safeguarding the professional capacity and status that you hold in the public domain and with considerations to the FSPs you represent. What you say on social media, directly or indirectly, and even when communicating (formally or informally) with clients, friends (and anyone else for that matter, even during general discussions) could jeopardise your future under the fit and proper requirements set out to uphold under the FAIS Act.

Google will always be a useful resource in terms of bringing yourself up to date and broadening your knowledge on cryptocurrencies and the blockchain, but be warned: finding reputable sources in places where fake news thrives can be tricky. I have spent considerable time researching cryptocurrencies and blockchain technology. From this base of knowledge, I published a series of articles that reflect my understanding of this phenomena from a financial advisor's point of view, and I have now written this book.

My hope is that this book will help you to answer and explain the technical aspects of digital currencies and blockchain to your clients, as well as get to the bottom of its associated risk concerns together with the possible opportunities they present. I therefore urge you to study this book, and, with my full permission, to freely share those aspects that you feel are appropriate with your clients and your networks. You can then walk away knowing that you have fulfilled your fiduciary duties and mitigated any Ombud's risks. It would be up to your clients to make the final decision, having been fully informed of all eventualities.

Now would be a good time with the permission of my good friend and respected financial professional and regulatory expert, Anton Swanepoel to share his thoughts on Bitcoin and other virtual currencies, in his capacity as Chair of The Financial Planning Committee of the FIA.

"Advisors, beware Bitcoin and other virtual currencies!"

Over the past fourteen years, South African financial advisors have been held accountable by the FAIS Ombud, the Appeal Board and our courts after advising clients on high-risk investments that failed. The question is whether history will repeat itself as more and more financial advisors buy into, and express "opinions" to their clients about virtual currencies such as Bitcoin, Darkcoin, Peercoin and Feathercoin.

The Financial Intermediaries Association of South Africa (FIA) is concerned about financial advisors expressing opinions about virtual currencies to clients (or potential clients) without understanding the potential implications. The Financial Planning Committee of the FIA has consulted the User Alert issued by National Treasury and the FIAS

Department of the Financial Services Board to obtain clarity on the risks for financial advisors.

The purpose of this article is to issue a firm warning to financial advisors. What follows are important aspects that advisors must consider, given the fact that virtual currencies have clearly become the new "flavour of the decade".

According to South Africa's National Treasury, while virtual currencies can be bought and sold on various platforms, they are not defined as securities in terms of the Financial Markets Act, 2012 (Act No. 19 of 2012). Bitcoin and other virtual currencies are not regulated, and Treasury has stated that there are no specific laws or regulations that address the use of virtual currencies and, consequently, no legal protection or recourse is afforded to users of virtual currencies.

A virtual currency is not a financial product as defined in section 1(1) of the FAIS Act, and the definition of "advice" has no relevance when it relates to a product that is not a financial product. However, although the FAIS Act does not apply to virtual currencies, it does not mean that a person (who is also an FSP) advising a client to invest in a virtual currency cannot be held liable, based on delict.

In our view, expressing an opinion, which is perceived by a client as an endorsement or encouragement to "buy" Bitcoin, for example, may attract liability for advisors. It is well-published that the High Court in the Eastern Cape previously held an advisor accountable for "giving advice at a braai", and advisors should therefore not be surprised if this happens again. It is fashionable for advisors to engage in these conversations, with some even encouraging their clients to attend Bitcoin presentations.

In the Oosthuizen and Marisa Vogel matter (Case number 2858/2012), the High Court in Bloemfontein stated that the principles in Durr v ABSA, (a matter that went all the way to the Supreme Court of Appeal and which preceded the FAIS Act by several years) is still relevant today. The Durr v ABSA case dealt with the duties of an advisor, which includes the duty to act with care, skill and diligence. The principles in this matter have been used by the FAIS Ombud and the High Court on many occasions as the legal basis on which advisors have been held liable in the past. Advisors would do well to consider it carefully.

The FAIS Ombud frequently issues determinations against advisors who do not understand the "product" that they have "sold".

Very few people, if any, can explain exactly how virtual currency works. According to Treasury, *"a virtual currency is a unit of account that is digitally or electronically created and stored. Members of the virtual community agree to accept these units as a representation of value in the same way that currency is accepted. In contrast to traditional currencies, virtual currencies operate without the authority of central banks, and are therefore not regulated. The price of virtual currencies is based on investor sentiment and can rise rapidly, thus attracting investors looking for very high returns from investments.*

However, the prices of virtual currencies tend to be very volatile and can drop as quickly as they rise. This may encourage speculative behaviour, which in turn spurs more volatility. Financial risks are, therefore, limitless and claims cannot be made for such losses."

One of the main arguments that the FAIS Ombud, the Appeal Board, and our courts have used in their findings against advisors, is the issue of due diligence. Currently, it is simply impossible to perform a due diligence on virtual currencies.

National Treasury, on behalf of the South African Reserve Bank, the Financial Services Board, the South African Revenue Service, and the Financial Intelligence Centre, has warned members of the public to be aware of the risks associated with the use of virtual currencies for either transactions or investments. Treasury has made it clear that there is no investor protection, and no recourse.

Furthermore, because virtual currencies are not regulated, users are not protected and are at the risk of losing money. This does not guarantee that financial advisors will not be held accountable if it is perceived that they have expressed an opinion which investors could claim to have persuaded them to buy into Bitcoin.

It is also important to remember that advisors do not have to be paid for their guidance for it to qualify as 'advice'. Being paid a fee or commission is not a prerequisite for accountability. Financial advisors who become involved in guiding clients in this area should, therefore, not be surprised if a client decides to hold them accountable. Neither should they expect any mercy from the FAIS Ombud, the Appeal Board or our courts if and when clients complain or institute legal action against them should they lose any of their money.

History may indeed repeat itself - again - if financial advisors are not extremely careful.

Anton Swanepoel CFP®

CHAPTER 14

FINAL OBSERVATIONS AND COMMENTS

I have to come to the logical conclusion that investing in Bitcoin and other cryptocurrencies would be purely speculative in nature at this stage of development of the crypto ecosystem.

The price will be driven up as long as the number of buyers outnumbers the sellers, and the price will move downwards when the sellers outnumber the buyers.

The way in which investors buy low and sell high during the volume adjustments between the number of sellers and buyers could make for good profits or poor losses. It does, however, require tremendous discipline to get in and out within the short windows of opportunity created by the massive volatility. It is usually at this point that human emotions kick in and the little devil on your shoulder makes you believe that there are even greater profits to be made on the way up, and if we sell out on the down that the losses would be less than we expect them to be.

The concern with Bitcoin is that unsophisticated investors are conned by Bitcoin 'experts' to buy into Bitcoin (without educating them) with the promise that it will result in significant profits and riches. Surely these investors would question why anyone would want to sell Bitcoins if they are as valuable as they are made out to be? Alas, no. Instead, the FOMO effect kicks in, and the herd buys in without performing any due diligence.

The biggest culprits appear to be the mining conglomerates who benefit either by way of price fluctuations or through remuneration for mining the Bitcoin blocks and authorising the transactions of Bitcoin owners.

Cryptocurrency is here to stay; that is a given. It has a useful purpose as a unit of exchange where merchants are willing to accept it as a currency, provided it has inherent stability. I am, however, of the opinion that instead of having multiple altcoins in circulation for this purpose that we should rather have a couple of dominant cryptocurrencies. These dominant currencies would become the real store-of-value, meeting the criteria of a currency per se, and allowing for mass merchant adoption through regulatory protection. Some of these dominant currencies could potentially be Bitcoin, Ethereum, Ripple and Litecoin, but only with significant design improvements, or there could be a completely new generation of coins in the future.

If this were the case, Bitcoin's value could be well above USD 100 000 (for one Bitcoin) in its fully-diluted stage (which would be when all 21 million coins mined by 2140), purely due to its 'finite scarcity', but that would be a long shot, and its developers would have to put an end to the rot and abuse of their beloved Bitcoin.

There is currently little indication of Bitcoin being adopted on a mass scale as a unit of exchange. As mentioned throughout this book, the mass adoption of Bitcoin has been as a speculative asset, which led to the massive volatility in price fluctuations as witnessed especially since January 2017, and even more so since January 2018.

The hope is that sanity will eventually prevail. This will only happen when the abuse of crypto leads to the bottom dropping out of the cryptocurrency market, followed by the cryptocurrency phoenix rising from the ashes in its intended form, leading to its mass adoption as a transaction tool by merchants and peer-to-peer platforms.

The belief that cryptocurrencies are a new asset class (referred to as crypto assets) that enable decentralised applications is problematic, and labelling it as such is an abuse of its intended use as a cryptocurrency or unit of exchange. As long as this propaganda is put out there, Bitcoin will continue to remain volatile. This volatility makes it impossible to classify Bitcoin as a unit of exchange.

There is also a question around whether a bubble would deplete the value of the bottom line of Bitcoin in its entirety, or not. This is unlikely to be the case if Bitcoin is used as a transactional payment system, since the miners incur costs in order to mine Bitcoins, and these costs must be recovered. Bitcoin's 'intrinsic' value only exists because of the cost that is perceived to be incurred by the miners to mine one Bitcoin Block and the coins within it.

Any cost above the mining cost is purely speculative, and more likely to exist during a bubble or a major correction. $8 000 would make the cost-efficiency of transactions impossible, but a cost of between $800 and $1 000 would be more practical.

In terms of decentralised services – a major propaganda tool for Bitcoin and crypto – I believe that the proof of this particular pudding will be evident over time.

Currently, the fact that these services are slower, more expensive, less scalable, have a poor user experience and are accompanied by massive volatility and uncertain governance, it may be the case that this particular pudding may not taste as good as its well established centralised counterparts.

I am always amazed by some of the propaganda I read on social media on crypto, when it is referred to as a mania or bubble,. The believers, in terms of their justification of Bitcoin, tend to state that 'it is rational to be irrational' during the initial stages of the crypto evolution. The Bitcoin naysayers are crushed by the believers and the evangelists on social media during Bitcoin's defensive propaganda awareness campaigns, even though Bitcoin believers have been unable to come up with any credible arguments in favour of Bitcoin.

It is interesting to note that when the price experienced a major correction as it did in January 2018, the naysayers grew louder and the believers became quiet. This is a phenomenon on its own, although it could be put down to nothing more than typical human behaviour.

If the prices of cryptocurrencies do not stabilise soon, then digital tokens could indeed end up being a bubble.

In January 2018, two Pittsburgh University researchers, Carey Caginalp and his father, Gunduz Caginalp, went out on a mission to find a way to determine Bitcoin's real value. After a significant amount of research, the bottom line of their findings was that an asset that has no value by traditional measures might already *be* in a bubble. They released a subsequent report later that month stating that "...the cryptocurrencies may simply be a mechanism for a transfer of wealth from the latecomers to the early entrants and nimble traders".

Forty percent of all Bitcoin is held by approximately one thousand people. These Bitcoin owners have significant sway over the price of the cryptocurrency and, as such, price manipulation is of grave concern, being extremely dangerous in a bubble environment.

So, is crypto a bubble (or not), or is crypto the making of a Fourth Industrial Revolution phenomenon? I believe that, at some stage, the blockchain (and similar technology) will most certainly be a significant part of the new industrial revolution and survive us beyond our current lifetimes.

In terms of crypto being a bubble, I believe that most cryptocurrencies are indeed in a bubble environment in their current forms, and that it is only those that transform into mass adoption tokens (instead of being used as speculative assets) that will survive the bubble impact and a threatening cryptomania implosion.

In final conclusion, I trust that this book, with its analysis of **'both sides of the coin'**, will help you to make an informed decision on cryptocurrencies and the blockchain and in one way or another, prevent you from getting caught up into the 'Cryptomania' of things. For those readers who are financial services industry professionals, I hope that you now find yourself armed with a wealth of information that will allow you to truly add value to your clients and your network.

ABOUT THE AUTHOR

Kobus Kleyn is a Certified Financial Planner and a Director at Kainos Financial Services. He obtained his Post Graduate Diploma in Financial Planning at the University of Free State (South Africa) and his MDP & AEP from UNISA. He holds many other qualifications.

He currently is Chairperson of the Financial Planning Institute (FPI) RDR Workgroup and the Liberty Ethics FA Committee. He is Vice-Chairperson of the FPI Client Engagement Committee. He also serves on the FPI Annual Convention Committee and the Million Dollar Round Table (MDRT) Task Forces. He has served on many past committees and task forces for the FPI, FIA (Financial Intermediaries Association) and MDRT over the years. He has been past-area and country chair for MDRT South Africa.

Kobus holds membership with the FPI (with the CFP designation); SAIT (South African Institute of Tax Practitioners, with the Tax Practitioner designation); FISA

(Fiduciary Institute of Southern Africa); STEP (Society of Trust and Estate Practitioner, with a TEP designation); FIA (The Financial Intermediaries Association of Southern Africa); IISA (The Insurance Institute of South Africa); The Institute of Ethics South Africa; and Unashamedly Ethical.

Kobus was the inaugural winner of the FPI "It starts with me" award in 2015, and went on to receive the award again in 2016. In 2017 he was awarded the FPI Media Award. Kobus was awarded the MDRT Leadership Award in 2014 and has been a Top of the Table MDRT member since 2012. He is a FPI, FIA and a MDRT Pro-Bono Volunteer, as well as a MDRT Foundation Silver Knight status holder.

Kobus has a true Passion for the Financial Services Profession and works purposefully with like-minded stakeholders to help transform the financial industry into a fully-fledged profession. He accomplishes this through the power of social and print media, presentations, workshops and talks.

Kobus has published over 200 articles in and on various media platforms and has been a speaker at the Annual MDRT Convention, FPI Annual Convention, and on several other platforms.

Kobus is rated in the top 1% on LinkedIn, with over 20 000 financial professionals connected to him globally. He uses LinkedIn as a platform to drive awareness to the financial services profession and his professional designations.

Kobus is a thought leader in many sectors including the financial services profession, in regulatory environments such as RDR, TCF Twin Peaks, on social Media, personal branding, Futuristic Leadership, Crypto Technology, and other disruptive Fintech subjects.

OTHER BOOKS BY KOBUS KLEYN

Kobus is the author of the book *Passion for the Profession - Mastering the 9 P's to Professionalism.*

Kobus' vision is to see the financial services industry transform into a fully-fledged profession with a common shared vision.

He has worked tirelessly to achieve this transformation through the sharing of best operational practices within the profession. This book, published in March 2017, was written for financial planning and advisory professionals (or those aspiring to be), across financials disciplines worldwide.

Based on his many years of personal experience, combined with learnings from his professional affiliations and his fellow financial planners, Kobus outlines a step-by-step process to transform the financial adviser from a "product-selling intermediary" into a financial planning professional through his nine P's, including, among others, a strong value *Proposition*, code of conduct, ethics and *Professionalism*, a *Personal brand* to be proud of, and proven methods to build *Passive income*.

Kobus is also the author of the book *RDR – Mastering Key Elements to RDR*.

The Retail Distribution Review (RDR) proposes significant regulatory reform. It is important that all financial service providers are able to understand, and comply with, the new requirements.

The book charts the transformative history of RDR from white paper stage through to the current RDR situation in South Africa. It encompasses the global pre-and-post RDR environments, and takes a close view of the current pre-RDR environment in South Africa, detailing RDRs transformation through a period of tough negotiations with the Financial Services Board (FSB) and other key industry stakeholders in South Africa.

This book is a roadmap that will bring financial stakeholders – including short-term-, healthcare-, and the long-term insurance sectors - up to date with RDR as it currently stands. It is a roadmap that will allow for rapid learning and education on RDR in South Africa, giving financial advisors a competitive edge by providing them with the tools they require in order to become RDR ready.

For more information:

Email: Kobus.kleyn@liblink.co.za

Mobile: 082-800-9136

Connect with Kobus on LinkedIn at:
https://www.linkedin.com/in/kobuskleynfinancialplanner

www.ingramcontent.com/pod-product-compliance
Lightning Source LLC
Chambersburg PA
CBHW052254220526
45471CB00001B/326